SMART TEACHING
STRONGER LEARNING

SMART TEACHING STRONGER LEARNING

Practical Tips From 10 Cognitive Scientists

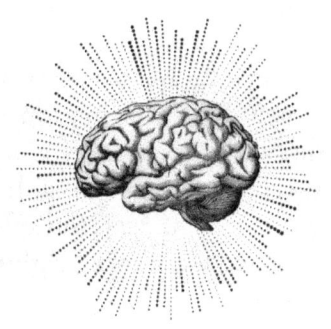

Edited by Pooja K. Agarwal, Ph.D.

Smart Teaching Stronger Learning: Practical Tips From 10 Cognitive Scientists

This book as a compendium of chapters is Copyright © 2025 by Pooja K. Agarwal. The individual chapters are Copyright © 2025 by their respective authors.

Published by Unleash Learning Press
An imprint of Unleash Learning LLC (Boston, MA)
www.retrievalpractice.org
ask@retrievalpractice.org

All rights reserved. Unleash Learning Press supports creativity, diverse voices, free expression, and the value of copyright. The purpose of copyright is to encourage writers to create vibrant works that enrich our culture.

The scanning, uploading, and distribution of this book without permission is theft of the authors' intellectual property. No part of this publication may be reproduced in any form or by any electronic or mechanical means, including information storage and retrieval systems, without permission in writing by the publisher, except for brief quotations. If you would like permission to use material from this book, contact the publisher at ask@retrievalpractice.org. Thank you for your support of the authors' rights by purchasing an authorized edition of this book.

The publisher is not responsible for websites or third-party content that are referred to in this publication.

ISBN (paperback): 979-8-9918191-0-7
ISBN (e-book): 979-8-9918191-1-4
Library of Congress Control Number: 2024924118

Cover Design: Yolande Sukal

Contributing Authors

Janell R. Blunt, Ph.D.
Associate Professor of Psychology
Anderson University (USA)

Shana K. Carpenter, Ph.D.
Professor of Psychology
Oregon State University (USA)

Roberta Ekuni, Ph.D.
Adjunct Professor of Psychology
Universidade Estadual de Londrina (Brazil)

Lisa K. Fazio, Ph.D.
Associate Professor of Psychology
Vanderbilt University (USA)

Cynthia L. Nebel, Ph.D.
Director of Learning Services
St. Louis University School of Medicine (USA)

Steven C. Pan, Ph.D.
Assistant Professor of Psychology
National University of Singapore (Singapore)

Michelle L. Rivers, Ph.D.
Assistant Professor of Psychology
Santa Clara University (USA)

Lisa K. Son, Ph.D.
Professor of Psychology
Barnard College (USA)

Kripa Sundar, Ph.D.
Founder and Lead Researcher
EdTech Recharge (USA)

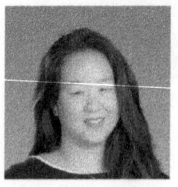
Veronica X. Yan, Ph.D.
Associate Professor of Psychology
The University of Texas at Austin (USA)

Contents

Introduction — 1

1. **Retrieval Practice** — 8
   Smart Teaching Strategies for Stronger Learning

2. **Early Childhood Education** — 20
   Retrieval-Based Learning for Children

3. **Spaced Practice** — 27
   Optimize Class Time to Boost Learning

4. **Interleaving** — 36
   Mix Things Up to Support Long-Term Learning

5. **Metacognition** — 46
   Monitoring, Control, and Trusting in the Self

6. **Concept Mapping** — 56
   Strengthen Learning with Linking Words

7. **The Effective Teaching Cycle** — 67
   Motivation, Scaffolding, and Reinforcement

8. **Transfer of Learning** — 75
   Foster Students' Application of Knowledge

9. **Bringing It Together** — 84
   Bite-Sized Adjustments for Powerful Engagement

10. **Neuromyths Debunked** — 95
    Why They Persist and How to Think Smarter

About the Editor — 103
Acknowledgments — 104
References — 106

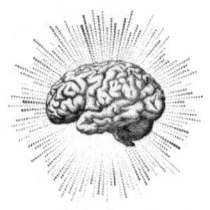

Introduction

Pooja K. Agarwal, Ph.D. (Editor)
Associate Professor of Psychology, Berklee College of Music

When I started my teacher training program in college, the pedagogy courses didn't have textbooks. I was very confused. Don't college courses have textbooks (in the early 2000s, at least)? I had, perhaps naively, imagined that effective teaching methods were grounded in research. My courses were taught by expert teachers, but without journal articles and books, so I had to take at face value that the "best" way to teach and the "best" way for students to learn were tried-and-true methods based on how teachers have always taught.

After taking more pedagogy courses, as well as psychology and neuroscience courses, I came to a not-so-comforting realization: Teaching and learning are complicated, so perhaps optimal methods for improvement simply don't exist. At the same time, I felt that learning how to drive a car, speak a new language, or solve an algebra problem are fundamentally the same human process: absorbing information, retaining it, and applying it.

In a Cognitive Psychology course, I discovered that scientists have been investigating learning for more than a century, and I devoured as much as I could about this field of research. I began shifting my teaching from merely presenting content to helping students remember and use what they were learning. With this new approach, my students became better equipped to engage in critical thinking and insightful discussion in a way that was incredibly fulfilling, far beyond what I ever imagined.

I felt so energized! I wanted educators to experience the career-changing lightbulb moment I had after integrating the science of learning with teaching. Suddenly, I had a sense of urgency to uncover, test, and refine effective teaching methods using rigorous research methods. Because as soon as we know what truly works best in education, the sooner we can transform student learning more profoundly than ever before.

Why This Book Exists

Over my 20-year career as a cognitive scientist, teacher, and author, I have witnessed monumental gains in the field of cognitive science in understanding how students learn, especially in real classroom environments. Educators are using evidence to improve their teaching, and the recent abundance of resources on the science of learning is astounding.

But there are still persistent misconceptions about learning and misguided recommendations for teachers based on so-called "research" that is outdated, obscure, or flawed. Educators need research-based teaching strategies they can trust and that's why I created *Smart Teaching Stronger Learning*: to share the science of learning straight from the source — researchers who are also teachers.

The 10 cognitive scientists featured in this book practice what they preach and they love sharing how they teach. Plus, they have done the heavy lifting for you by translating research, developing class activities, and testing them out in their own classrooms. You'll read about their innovative teaching strategies, and you'll find comfort knowing that many of the strategies you already use are backed by research.

I also wanted to create a book about the science of learning that's clear and easy to digest. As someone who strives to improve, but lacks time to find effective teaching strategies and implement them, I designed *Smart Teaching Stronger Learning* with curious and busy educators in mind.

As a *curious* educator, you already spend considerable time and energy thinking about learning. Perhaps you are a pre-service teacher looking to start your career, or you are a veteran teacher who wants to refresh your approach. You might be a faculty member at a teaching center or a graduate student conducting research. For educators from all walks of life, this book is a guide to thinking about learning in a new light, with some bite-sized research along the way.

In addition to being curious, you're also a *busy* educator. Trust me, I've been there. I know what it's like to juggle lesson planning, grading, emails, and meetings (not to mention the actual teaching). That's why this book is intentionally short — only 10 pages per chapter — and also why each author focuses on teaching strategies you can implement immediately, without additional course prep or grading.

Whether you teach K–12 students or graduate students, or you're new to teaching or a long-time educator: If you want to improve student learning, this book is for you.

The Scary "R" Word: Research

When I started working on this book, I polled a few of my teacher friends about potential titles. There was a clear consensus: People are intimidated by the word "research" and the phrase "evidence-based" has become a cliché. That's why I decided on *Smart Teaching Stronger Learning*. The first half of the title, *Smart Teaching*, highlights how you'll be better informed about cognitive science after reading this book. The second half, *Stronger Learning*, emphasizes the ultimate outcome: strengthening long-term learning with strategies proven to raise student achievement.

Even though the words research and evidence-based aren't in the title (thank you, friends!), you might feel nervous about reading a book by scientists. That makes sense — I don't always love scientific writing, either. I want to reassure you that this book doesn't include statistics, complicated theoretical arguments, or unapproachable research by out-of-touch academics. What this book *does* include is real solutions to real problems by down-to-earth teachers who conduct research on learning.

You are a teacher who also conducts research on learning. As a teacher-scientist, you engage in research in your school or classroom. You conduct experiments to see what works (and what doesn't work). For example, you've probably experimented with how to start a lesson to capture students' attention, how to write exam questions that aren't too easy or too hard, or how to adjust class activities that take longer than you expect. Even if you don't have formal training in how to conduct research, you ask questions and seek answers — and that's what makes you a teacher-scientist.

Rather than thinking of *Smart Teaching Stronger Learning* as a book about research (scary!), think of it as a book about questions (mystery and intrigue!). Here are some questions you may have pondered that are answered in this book:

- Why do my students keep forgetting everything I teach them, no matter what I do?

- Why is it that my students seem to understand a concept, but then they struggle to apply what they've learned?

- How can I improve students' skill-based learning, like writing and math?

- How can I tell the difference between a teaching fad versus a strategy that's based on legitimate research?

Remember: This book was written *for* teachers *by* teachers (who happen to be scientists). The authors share practical classroom tips drawn from their area of expertise without jargon or nonsense. I promise: You've got this.

Ten Voices in Cognitive Science

The cognitive scientists included in this book are representative of today's educators, not the traditional stereotype of scientists (Google "draw a scientist" for a fascinating classroom activity related to widespread perceptions of scientists). As women, BIPOC, LGBTQ+, first generation college graduates, English language learners, and educators who have taught students from historically marginalized communities, these cognitive scientists know what it's like to teach in the real world.

In addition, the contributors in this book conduct research in real classrooms. Cognitive science research dates back to the late 1800s and most of it was conducted in carefully controlled laboratory environments with basic learning materials, like word pairs and pictures of household objects. We know that classrooms aren't carefully controlled. Of course, they're the opposite: messy, hectic, and loud. I'm proud that the scientists included in this book are actively partnering with educators and publishing the newest classroom research, adding to our understanding of how learning works "in the wild."

I can personally vouch for each scientist. They have conducted some of the highest-cited research in our field and they are genuinely dedicated to improving education. But as Levar Burton said on *Reading Rainbow*, "You don't have to take my word for it." At the end of each chapter, I've included links to the author's website and social media, and I encourage you to reach out to them. Don't be scared; cognitive scientists are fascinated by learning, so you already have something in common. Ask for more information about their teaching strategies, explore opportunities to have them collaborate with your school, and brainstorm how to conduct research in your classroom.

How to Read This Book

Read this book in any order you want and feel free to skip around. As a curious educator, find the chapter that looks the most relevant for you. As a busy educator, skim and look for teaching strategies listed with bullet points. If you'd like to learn more about a topic or you want to read some research, each chapter includes two carefully selected further readings, with a detailed list of references at the end of the book (you can typically access research articles for free via https://scholar.google.com by searching for the title).

I'd like to offer a few learning objectives to guide your reading:

By the end of this book, you should know:

- Foundational principles about how students learn
- Key findings from the field of cognitive science
- Effective teaching strategies and why they improve long-term learning

By the end of this book, you should be able to:

- Adjust your pedagogy to strengthen students' long-term learning
- Articulate and speak about the science of learning with colleagues and students
- Think critically about what successful teaching and learning mean to you

Final Thoughts

Teaching is becoming more complex and more challenging every day. In the face of emerging world events and advancements (a global pandemic, political unrest, and artificial intelligence, just to name a few), education is taking a form we have never seen before.

While reading this book, I challenge you to focus on the most basic element of education: learning. When you strengthen your students' learning, they will forget less and achieve more. Your students will grow to become independent, thoughtful thinkers in this ever-changing world. They will ask questions and seek answers. And you have the expertise to make that happen.

About the Editor

Dr. Pooja K. Agarwal (she/her) is an Associate Professor of Psychology at the Berklee College of Music in Boston, Massachusetts. Dr. Agarwal teaches courses on introductory psychology, cognitive psychology, and social psychology. She is the lead author of the book *Powerful Teaching: Unleash the Science of Learning* and her award-winning research on how students learn has been featured in *The New York Times*, *Education Week*, *Scientific American*, and *NPR*. She earned her Ph.D. from Washington University in St. Louis.

Learn more about Dr. Agarwal at https://retrievalpractice.org/agarwal, follow her on various social media platforms at @RetrieveLearn, and subscribe for her newsletter at https://retrievalpractice.org/subscribe.

1

Retrieval Practice

Smart Teaching Strategies for Stronger Learning

Janell R. Blunt, Ph.D.
Associate Professor of Psychology, Anderson University

Taylor was in tears. We had just finished the first exam in my introductory psychology class, a required class at my university. Back row dwellers, athletes, non-majors, even high school students — I had them all. On this particular exam, Taylor scored a 70%, a solid 15% below the class average. Taylor smiled through the tears and said, "I've never passed an exam before. This is the first time and it's because of retrieval practice."

I have plenty of stories of students who went from a C to A or even from an A to an A+ after engaging in retrieval practice. One of my students literally bounced in their chair with delight after getting a 100% on an exam exclaiming, "Retrieval works! Retrieval works!"

An Energizing Strategy for All Learners

Retrieval practice is the mental process of bringing previously learned information to mind. Every time you use your memory to "retrieve" something you learned before and think about it now, you're using retrieval practice. Recalling the name of a new coworker you just met or writing about your day in a journal are ways you may use retrieval practice without even realizing it.

In the classroom, when a student actively recalls information from memory rather than passively reviewing it or relying on notes, they strengthen their learning. An example of a simple retrieval-based activity is called a *brain dump*. A brain dump (known as "free recall" in the scientific literature) involves having students write about what they learned in class from memory, just like journaling about one's day from memory.

In my 20 years of conducting research on learning, I've found that retrieval practice boosts learning not just for high-achieving, motivated students, but also for students with a wide range of abilities and motivation levels. From teaching in large lecture halls packed with over 500 students to conducting retrieval-based research in elementary school classrooms, I've seen all types of students benefit from retrieval practice. I've also combed through experiment after experiment conducted in real classrooms to find out when and for whom retrieval practice is beneficial. The answer? All of the time and for everyone. From spelling, mathematics, science, history, and psychology, to skills like CPR or even dental diagnosis, retrieval practice is an effective strategy for increasing student learning.[1]

The great news is that you can start using retrieval practice in the classroom without extra preparation, class time, or cost. Plus, you're probably already using retrieval practice. In one survey, 100% of teachers reported integrating retrieval practice into their teaching, with two out of three teachers using it in every lesson.[2] The majority of teachers report using short answer questions or low-stakes quizzes to practice retrieval, and my goal is to give you additional ways to transform your classroom into an energizing, retrieval-based learning environment you and your students will love.

White Boards

I have an old suitcase full of small white boards and dry erase markers that I bring to my introductory psychology class every day. Students know to grab a white board before heading to their desks, which are grouped in pods with five other students.

Rather than starting class by reviewing a previous lesson, simply ask students to retrieve information by writing answers to questions you ask on their white boards. These questions can be ones you've made in advance or ones you think of on the spot if you notice students struggling to understand a concept or stay focused. Here are some question prompts you can try with white boards:

- **Brain Dump**: Start or end each class with a brain dump by asking students to retrieve as much as they remember for 2 minutes. Alternatively, ask students to retrieve 3 key points from class. No prep or grading required.

- **Rapid Retrieval**: Every 10 minutes or so, ask a question about a topic you've covered. Have students show you their white boards once they've written the answer. Help yourself remember it's time for a rapid retrieval by adding a picture of a golden retriever a few times in your lecture slides.

- **Application of Knowledge**: Have students apply concepts by creating their own examples. In my class on personality psychology, students make a list of Disney characters who exemplify different personality traits like extroversion or agreeableness, such as Olaf from the movie *Frozen* because he is talkative and always eager to make new friends. Students then show their examples to their pod, who guess the related concept for even more retrieval practice.

- **Drawings**: Ask students to draw an image that describes concepts from the lesson. Students then share and guess the concept, without looking at their notes or textbook. I've had students draw neurons, brains, charts, and tables. There are endless possibilities of using drawings as a retrieval format.

White Boards: Why They Work

White boards provide flexibility for the types of question prompts you can ask. Plus, white boards give students the opportunity to retrieve what they've learned in different formats: images, words, tables, phrases, etc. While there is no conclusive evidence that students benefit from having lessons that are taught in the way that match their preferred learning style (which is a great relief for us as educators; see also Chapter 10), students have preferences and white boards enable students to demonstrate their variety of strengths.[3]

In addition, students just really enjoy white boards. Something about having an eraser on hand normalizes mistakes and eases student anxiety. Mistakes are ok — just erase it and retrieve it again. By having students constantly retrieving or sharing retrieval responses with peers, they'll also learn to help each other out — much like team building exercises, but without a competitive environment.

And if you have a small classroom or white boards on the wall, consider flipping your classroom: Have students read the textbook or watch an online lecture *before* class, leaving the entire class period free for you and your students to practice retrieval. Students can spend the entire class period standing at the white board retrieving questions and topics. When I changed my neuroscience class to include this format one day per week, exam grades improved by 20% and students became much more engaged and passionate about neuroscience.

I have found that using white boards for retrieval practice fits a range of budgets and time constraints. Fortunately, packs of individual white boards that come with markers and erasers are surprisingly inexpensive. You can also cut costs by creating your own white boards by putting blank pages of paper with cardstock into sheet protectors and cutting erasers out of scrap pieces of fleece fabric.

White Boards: What to Watch Out For

- **Not starting early enough**: For best results, introduce retrieval activities on the first day of class. Set the expectation that you want to hear from students early and often, and they will quickly learn to participate.

- **Students relying on notes**: Emphasize the importance of trying the activity without notes. When you first introduce any retrieval activity, especially white boards at their desk, monitor students to ensure they aren't simply copying notes. Stress that difficult learning is learning that lasts and that mistakes are okay.

- **Students not participating if you use paper**: If you test this method with paper instead of white boards, don't expect as much buy-in from students. Students enjoy the novelty of white boards, and my students are delighted when I come to class wheeling my suitcase full of 60 white boards.

- **Too much social pressure**: When having students retrieve at the front of the classroom with white boards on the wall, some students might initially feel anxious to get started. The first time you introduce this retrieval method, try a silly retrieval prompt or trivia fact to create a supportive environment. Avoid assigning points for correct responses. While retrieval practice might seem scary, research shows it reduces anxiety for most students over time.[4]

- **Standing doesn't work for everyone**: If you're using white boards on the wall, be sure to have a plan for students who may not be able to stand for long periods of time. Have an equally appealing option like a stool or smaller white board you can provide to a seated student.

Clickers

To decrease mind wandering during class and improve learning with retrieval practice, I recommend using clickers. These student response systems are interactive handheld remotes that allow students to respond to questions individually. For a low-tech option, have students vote with their body (stand if you think A, sit if you think B; hold up one finger for option one, two for option two, etc.) or hold up premade colored index cards that correspond to different answer options.

Try using clickers to break up a content-heavy lecture session, which also gives you a glimpse into the minds of your students with instant feedback on their understanding (also known as formative assessment). You can seamlessly integrate quick clicker questions into your lesson to provide powerful boosts in learning without needing additional time.

When deciding how to include questions during your lessons or lectures, consider whether your goal is retrieval practice, comprehension, or connection:

Use Clickers for Retrieval Practice

Add a question several minutes after you've covered something new or replace your daily recap with a retrieval question from the previous day. Keep a handful of retrieval questions from any previous lesson in your back pocket for the end of a class period if you have a couple extra minutes of class time. Retrieval is so powerful that you can even use it *before* students have learned the material. I start my lesson on neuroscience by showing students a diagram of a neuron with an arrow pointing to an unlabeled part. I ask students to guess what that part is called. Initial performance is incredibly low (we haven't discussed neurons yet), but they always score highly on a similar exam question weeks later.

Use Clickers for Comprehension and Application

Immediately after teaching a concept, ask an applied question to assess if students can use the information in new situations, or give an inference question to get them connecting the new information to other topics from class. For example, after I introduce the topic of operant conditioning (punishment and reinforcement) in my introductory psychology class, I immediately give a scenario that requires students to apply how car manufacturers increase seat belt buckling behavior (the answer is negative reinforcement; the annoying ding a car makes stops once you buckle up).

Use Clickers to Connect with Everyday Life

Use clickers to poll students about how they feel about the lesson. For example, in a lesson on the importance of sleep, I begin by asking students to share how much they sleep. Before a lesson on the benefits of journaling, students share if they journal. Before a lesson on remembering names, students share whether they feel like they are bad at remembering names. Connecting new knowledge to your students' lives is another great way to improve learning.

Clickers: Why They Work

With clickers, you will target all levels of learning from foundational knowledge to higher level thinking, such as application, synthesis, and evaluation of content from prior lessons. Students benefit from immediate feedback via clickers without extra grading for you. You'll also gain more control of your teaching as you get in-the-moment pulse checks, which will allow you to speed up if something has been easily understood or put on the brakes if a concept didn't land. Because each student has their own clicker, student engagement will be near 100% rather than leaving you to rely on very extroverted or enthusiastic students.

Clickers: What to Watch Out For

- **Distractions using mobile apps**: There are many ed tech apps that allow students to use their phones or computers to respond to questions. This may seem convenient, but apps can also introduce distractions. In one college classroom study, students using their laptops had little self-awareness of how off-task they were, both when using their own laptops and when other students were off-task.[5]
- **Students not participating**: If students have clickers that are randomly handed out during class, they may not participate. To avoid this, assign each student a clicker number. This

allows you to see how individual students are doing before they take a graded quiz. It can also help you have a conversation with students about their engagement in class.

- **Student anxiety with points**: Assigning points for correct answers can lead to anxiety. Students may also become concerned with losing points if clicker responses weren't received. For this reason, I do not recommend assigning any points for clicker questions.

- **Clickers can be expensive**: Clicker remotes require some upfront costs and they are considered by some to be outdated technology, but they eliminate distractions and encourage participation. Index cards reduce distraction, but they also reduce the ease with which you get feedback. In my experience, using index cards led to less enthusiasm and participation than using clicker remotes.

Shift to a Retrieval Mindset

Implementing retrieval practice in the classroom is fairly straightforward; you don't need to reinvent your classroom or change everything you're doing. Instead, reinvent your *mindset*. Almost any activity can become a retrieval activity. Here are common teaching activities you might already use and how you can make small mindset shifts to boost student learning:

Textbook Reading

When students are asked how they study, most students say they re-read their textbooks. But this strategy merely boosts their confidence, while leaving them with very little lasting learning. It's shocking and discouraging how much students forget after just a couple days when they've learned something by re-reading.

Test this for yourself: can you draw the Apple logo? Which way is the leaf facing? Is there a bite in the apple? Which side is it on?

Does the apple have a smooth or bumpy bottom? If you're like most people, this is a very familiar logo — one you've looked at over and over again. But if you could picture it accurately, you're in a small minority of people. Only 1 out of 85 people can do this.[6] Looking at the logo repeatedly isn't enough to produce learning, just like re-reading over and over again doesn't produce learning.[7]

Teach students to practice retrieval by using headers in their textbook as retrieval cues. Once they've tried to remember and retrieve what the paragraph was about using the header, then — and only then — go back and re-read. To make re-reading an effective strategy, it must be used *after* retrieval practice as a form of feedback. Index cards or blank sheets of paper placed over the paragraph are a great way to stay accountable and not peak at the text too soon. Students can retrieve out loud to a parent, a peer, or to themselves by typing or handwriting responses.

Flashcards

Flashcards are quite popular. However, I rarely see them used well. To get the most out of flashcards, students must actually retrieve the information rather than flipping the card over and assuming they know the information. Teach students to say information out loud before flipping the card over or they can work with a partner to keep them accountable. Once a student is able to correctly retrieve the information, they shouldn't discard it right away. Instead, they can add it to a separate pile and shuffle the order for retrieval on a different day (see Chapters 3 and 4 on spaced practice and interleaving). As a rule of thumb based on research, aim for three correct retrievals on three different days.

Concept Mapping

Concept maps are visual representations of knowledge that involve connecting concepts with linking words and phrases (see Chapter 6). Traditionally, concept maps are made with the text in front of students. When I started conducting research as an undergraduate student, I wanted to know if retrieval practice could be better than a study strategy as popular as concept mapping. So, with the help of my research advisor, we designed a series of experiments to put retrieval to the test. The results were clear: Retrieval practice was a far superior method for learning compared to concept mapping.[8]

But this doesn't mean concept maps aren't effective. In a follow up set of experiments, we found that concept maps were just as effective when used as *retrieval maps*. Simply taking away the text from concept maps brought learning up to the same level as paragraph-based retrieval.[9] I've also used retrieval maps to help scaffold learning both in an elementary classroom and in the research lab by having students fill in partially completed maps.

Have students create retrieval maps from memory, either individually or in small groups. Scaffold their learning by giving students maps with missing concepts or phrases and have them finish it — something I've done in both my research and in my own classroom with great success.

Collaborative Games

I've used a variety of games to encourage low-stakes retrieval practice without time pressure or fear of disappointing teammates. Students in my class developed *Retrieval Tic Tac Toe*. To play, start by drawing a tic tac toe grid on the board. Split the class into two teams, each writing five questions for retrieval practice. One team asks a question while the other team collaborates to come up with an answer. If correct, they place an X on the grid. Teams then switch roles, with the other team now asking a question and placing an O if they answer correctly. Continue alternating turns, making the game an engaging and anxiety-free way to practice retrieval.

Final Thoughts

Taylor's story at the beginning of this chapter, along with 100+ years of research by cognitive scientists, are testaments to the power of implementing simple yet effective retrieval practice strategies that significantly boost students' long-term learning. Don't worry about whether you are having students retrieve in the "best" way. When my colleagues and I analyzed 50 classroom experiments looking for the very best ways to practice retrieval, we found that across grade levels, content areas, test delays, and feedback timing, retrieval practice works.[10] Any retrieval is the right retrieval.

Making the switch to retrieval-based learning doesn't need to involve a lot of initial set up, but it does involve discipline. Watch out for perfectionistic tendencies and help encourage students to set aside materials and see what they know. Don't punish incorrect answers and encourage the class to help each other out when a student gets an answer wrong. Soon, you'll have a classroom full of engaged students eager to learn and support each other.

As educators, our jobs are both challenging and rewarding. My hope for you is that your classroom will be filled with energy and curiosity as you develop and implement a variety of retrieval practice strategies that work with your age level and lesson content. And in addition to stronger learning for your students, may you find renewed energy and passion for teaching with retrieval-based strategies as I have. So, here's to retrieval practice!

Further Reading

Agarwal, P. K., Nunes, L. D., & Blunt, J. R. (2021). Retrieval practice consistently benefits student learning: A systematic review of applied research in schools and classrooms. *Educational Psychology Review, 33*, 1409–1453.

Karpicke, J. D., & Blunt, J. R. (2011). Retrieval practice produces more learning than elaborative studying with concept mapping. *Science, 331*(6018), 772–775.

About the Author

Dr. Janell Blunt (she/her) is an Associate Professor of Psychology at Anderson University near Indianapolis, Indiana. Dr. Blunt teaches courses on introductory psychology, cognitive psychology, research methods, and statistics. She has published numerous research articles on learning in top peer-reviewed journals, including the prestigious journal *Science*, and her work has been featured in *The New York Times*. Dr. Blunt is also a LinkedIn Learning instructor, where she shares evidence-based strategies and tips on how to learn in her course, entitled *Strategies to Learn and Upskill More Effectively*. She earned her Ph.D. from Purdue University.

Learn more about Dr. Blunt at https://retrievalpractice.org/blunt and follow her on LinkedIn at https://linkedin.com/in/janellblunt.

2

Early Childhood Education

Retrieval-Based Learning for Children

Lisa K. Fazio, Ph.D.
Associate Professor of Psychology, Vanderbilt University

One of the best ways to promote long-lasting learning is to have students retrieve key concepts from memory. Activities such as brain dumps, flashcards, and quizzes all require students to recall information. Importantly, these retrieval-based learning activities improve learning more than activities that do not require retrieval such as re-reading a text, viewing a completed concept map, or listening to a summary of the lesson. Retrieval-based learning also promotes learning and transfer in a variety of domains, including STEM subjects, social sciences, and foreign languages.

The benefits from retrieval practice are well established for both adolescents and adults, in the laboratory and in the classroom. But do younger children also benefit from retrieval practice? Based on emerging literature for preschool and elementary school students, there is clear evidence that retrieval practice improves learning in children.[1] Retrieval practice helps preschoolers learn the names of stuffed animals,[2] improves second graders' spelling performance,[3] and boosts third graders ability to learn the meaning of new vocabulary words.[4] Asking children questions about previously experienced events (e.g., a recent magic show or a classroom workshop) improves their memory for the experience.[5,6]

In fact, even infants benefit from retrieval practice. Three-month-olds who learned how to make a hanging mobile move by kicking their legs remembered the action for 14 days if they practiced the activity from memory, but they only remembered how to make the mobile move for 9 days if they simply watched someone else move the mobile.[7] Similarly, toddlers who were taught new action sequences (e.g., take a clown toy out of the chest, put it in a rocking chair, and rock it) remembered more actions 12 weeks after learning if they had the chance to retrieve the actions compared to watching a video of the action sequences.[8]

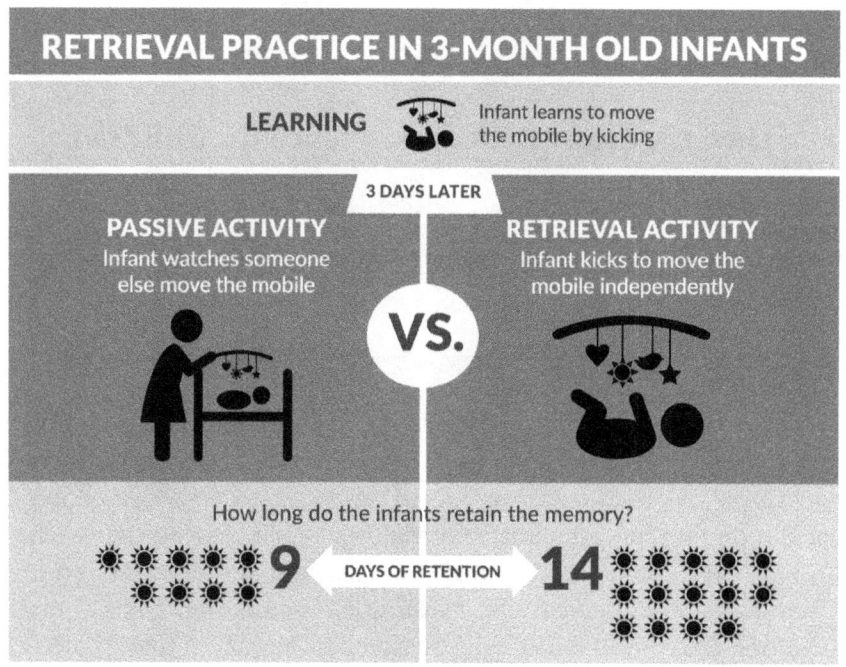

These are just a few demonstrations of children benefiting from retrieval-based learning early in life and the benefits occur for a wide age range of children. Here are more specific findings based on cognitive science research:

- Kindergartners better remembered the locations for objects following retrieval practice compared to when the experimenter showed them the locations.[9]
- Third graders who read about the sun remembered more information on a test one week later compared to when they re-read the passage.[10]
- Fifth graders better remember definitions of science concepts following retrieval-based learning with feedback.[11]

All of these examples show that younger children, just like adolescents and adults, benefit from opportunities to retrieve information from memory.

How to Adjust Retrieval Practice for Children

While retrieval-based learning can be beneficial for students of all ages, some additional adjustments will help ensure success for younger children:

Scaffolding

Provide scaffolding to help young children remember information during retrieval practice. When children do not benefit from retrieval-based learning, it is often because they were unable to retrieve any of the relevant information. With scaffolding, teachers can help students to recall more information (see Chapter 7 on the effective teaching cycle). For example, instead of asking broad questions like, "What do you remember about sloths?," provide scaffolded prompts such as, "What do you remember about how sloths move?" or "What do you remember about what sloths eat?"

In one study, when children ages 9–11 were asked to remember as much as they could from a science passage they had just read, they were only able to recall 7% of the key ideas and retrieval practice was not beneficial. However, when the students were given scaffolded questions about the passage (e.g., "Fog is made of what type of cloud?" and "describe the shape and color of stratus clouds"), retrieval practice increased their later memory for the information.[12]

Feedback

Provide feedback after errors to solidify accurate recall. Feedback is especially important when children are unable to retrieve the correct information. Trying to retrieve information, but failing, can still be useful if students receive feedback.[13] Numerous studies with adults show that guessing incorrectly and then being told the correct answer is more beneficial than simply studying the correct answer. Recent evidence suggests that the same is true with children. Both kindergartners and second graders benefited from guessing incorrectly before being told the correct answer. In this specific study, preschoolers saw no benefits, but they were also not harmed by their incorrect responses.[14]

While it can be useful, feedback is not always necessary for children to learn from retrieval practice. Children show benefits from retrieval-based learning, even without feedback, as long as students are able to retrieve some correct information during retrieval practice.

Desirable Difficulties

When deciding how to use retrieval-based learning with elementary school students, it can be useful to think through the idea of *desirable difficulties*. Desirable difficulties are activities that are effortful and may cause students to struggle, but they improve long-term learning of the information. Retrieval-based learning is a great example of a desirable difficulty; retrieval is effective when students have to struggle to remember the information, but they are still able to do so. Students learn less when retrieval practice is very easy or very difficult. The key is to aim for the "sweet spot" when retrieval is challenging, but successful.

Related to scaffolding, broad open-ended questions (e.g., "What have we learned about the solar system?") can make retrieval practice too difficult for younger children, but it is also possible to make retrieval practice too easy. Multiple studies have shown that children benefit more from retrieval practice when it occurs after they have forgotten some of the information, also called spaced practice (see Chapter 3). To find a sweet spot with desirable difficulties, consider asking students to recall how to multiply fractions one day or one week after the lesson, instead of having them recall it immediately after learning the information.

Cognitive-Processing Language

"Teacher talk" that includes learning strategy suggestions and metacognition questions that make students think about their own learning can be very beneficial for young learners (see also Chapter 5 about metacognition). Described as *cognitive-processing language* by researchers, exposure to this type of teacher talk improves students' memory abilities and their classroom learning. Here are examples of cognitive-processing language:

- "Who knows the first step we take when building a new structure?" (retrieving a procedure)

- "If you are having trouble thinking of ways to connect the wheel and axle, you can look at the diagram to help you." (strategy suggestions)

- "How did you figure out which pieces you would need to build a sturdy structure?" (thinking about thinking)

Cognitive-processing language seems to be particularly important for strategic problem solving. Researchers have shown that first graders in classrooms with frequent cognitive-processing language are more likely to use complex memory strategies at the end of the year than students in classrooms that were low in cognitive-processing language. In addition, young children in an afterschool program learned more strategies for building Lego cars when they were taught using cognitive-processing language.[15,16]

Final Thoughts

Retrieval-based learning is a powerful tool for increasing student learning. While most research in cognitive science has been conducted with adolescents and adults, recent work suggests that younger children also benefit from retrieval-based learning. For younger children, the key is to make retrieval practice challenging, but also successful.

Younger children may struggle to retrieve information in response to broad questions, so teachers should scaffold retrieval by asking more specific questions. Resist the temptation to make the task too easy because some struggle is useful. In addition, providing feedback is a great way to ensure that all children, not just those who were able to retrieve the correct information, benefit from retrieval practice. Overall, retrieval practice is an effective way to boost learning for students of all ages — even infants!

Further Reading

Fazio, L. K. & Marsh, E. J. (2019). Retrieval-based learning in children. *Current Directions in Psychological Science, 28*(2), 111–118.

Karpicke, J. D., Blunt, J. R., Smith, M. A., & Karpicke, S. S. (2014). Retrieval-based learning: The need for guided retrieval in elementary school children. *Journal of Applied Research in Memory and Cognition, 3*(3), 198–206.

About the Author

Dr. Lisa Fazio (she/her) is an Associate Professor of Psychology at Vanderbilt University in Nashville, Tennessee. Dr. Fazio teaches courses on cognitive psychology, developmental psychology, and misinformation. Her research focuses on how children and adults learn true and false information from the world around them, and on how to correct errors in people's knowledge. Dr. Fazio received the Early Career Impact Award from the Federation of Associations in Behavioral & Brain Sciences and the Frank Research Prize in Public Interest Communications. She earned her Ph.D. from Duke University.

Learn more about Dr. Fazio at https://retrievalpractice.org/fazio and follow her on Bluesky at @LKFazio.

3

Spaced Practice

Optimize Class Time to Boost Learning

Shana K. Carpenter, Ph.D.
Professor of Psychology, Oregon State University

Conventional wisdom tells us that the key to mastery is to spend more time learning; if your student performs poorly on an exam, they are likely to spend more time studying for the next one. And if you notice your students struggling to grasp a difficult concept, it makes sense to spend more time teaching that concept. But is more time spent studying and teaching better for learning?

Surprisingly, not always. Research reveals that the key to successful learning is *not* the total time spent learning, but the *way* in which that studying and teaching time is used.[1] In this chapter, I discuss how to use *spaced practice* to improve learning without changing the amount of time spent learning. Spaced practice is supported by hundreds of studies and over a century of research. It is simple and easy to implement, it works for any type of learning, and it improves students' long-term learning.

Research on Spaced Practice

Spaced practice (also called *spacing*) involves strategically arranging time spent learning into multiple sessions that are spread out over time. This can be compared to the more popular approach — known by many as cramming — in which students do most or all of their studying in one long session shortly before an exam.[2,3]

For example, in preparation for a Spanish exam, a student might study 50 vocabulary words by repeatedly trying to retrieve the English translation for Spanish words (e.g., Zapato – Shoe). Let's say the student goes through the whole list three times retrieving the translations the night before the exam. An alternative approach is to practice retrieving the list of vocabulary words on three separate occasions: a week before the exam, again a few days later, and again a few days after that. Both approaches involve the same amount of time learning, but they differ in how that time is scheduled.

Research shows that simply spacing out learning opportunities across multiple days leads to much higher achievement than learning the same amount of information all in one session. In one classroom study, middle school students retrieved information from their science lessons either right after the lessons ended or a few days after the lessons. On exams given at the end of the semester a few months later, students performed better when retrieval practice was spaced a few days after the lessons instead of right afterwards.[4]

In research I conducted with colleagues, middle school students answered questions about information from their history class either soon after they learned the material or several weeks after they learned it. When both groups were given an unexpected test nine months later, the group that reviewed after several weeks scored significantly higher.[5] Maintaining knowledge over the course of a semester or after a nine-month interval — equivalent to an academic year at many schools — shows that learning information through spaced practice leads to long-lasting and durable learning over time.

In another research study, high school students learned French vocabulary words back-to-back on the same day for 30 minutes (massed practice), or once per day over three days for 10 minutes each (spaced practice). Several days after the exercises were completed, all of the students were given an unannounced test.

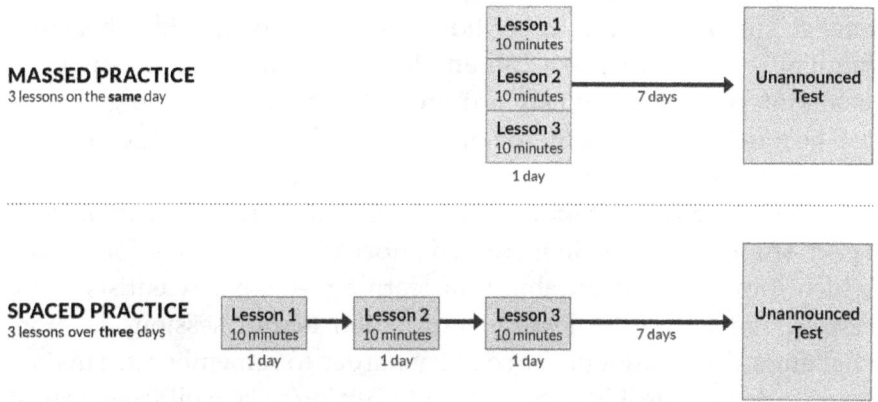

Contrary to what you might expect, students who completed the exercises with spaced practice across three days performed better (75%) than students who completed the exercises with massed practice on the same day (55%).[6] In other words, even though the two groups of students spent the same amount of time learning the material, the group that spaced out their practice over multiple days learned French significantly better.

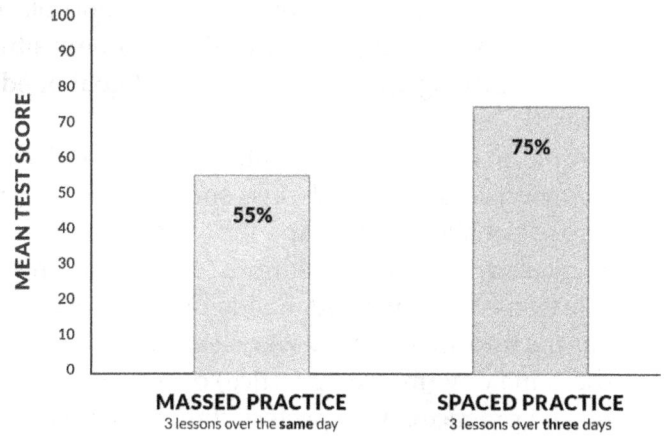

Why Spacing Works

Cramming increases the amount of information in short-term memory, but it does not improve long-term memory. When students engage in immediate repetition, information quickly becomes familiar — what scientists call an *illusion of knowing*. Unfortunately, when information is quickly acquired, it's often quickly forgotten. It can be much more difficult to remember the information after a week, or even a day.

On the other hand, when learning opportunities are spaced apart, students engage in increased effort to retrieve the information, which improves the durability of learning — what scientists call a *desirable difficulty*. Retrieving information across sessions is more challenging and students have to try harder to remember it. This can lead students to feel like they are not learning very well from spaced practice, but that's precisely why spacing works: The challenge from spacing significantly improves long-term learning.

Spacing Improves Transfer of Knowledge

Spaced practice improves students' long-term learning of academic knowledge and skills in a variety of subject areas, including language, math, science, and social studies.[7] Students who engage in spaced practice learn concepts better and show enhanced understanding — not just memorization — of how concepts apply to new situations. Being able to apply knowledge to a new situation is known as *transfer of learning* and it is an important goal of education (see also Chapter 8).

For example, in one study, elementary school children learned scientific information about food chains, such as the tendency for larger animals to eat smaller animals and the tendency for the number of species to increase when they have more food to eat. The children received four lessons that involved hands-on demonstrations and questions about the information they were learning. The four lessons occurred on the same day (massed practice) or once per week across four weeks (spaced practice). As expected, children who received the once-per-week spaced lessons learned the information better than children who received the lesson all in one day (see Chapter 2 about retrieval practice in early childhood education).[8]

In addition, on a later test over what they had learned, the spaced group performed better on questions over the basic concepts (for example, "Bigger animals typically eat ____ animals"), simple transfer questions ("What does the frog eat?"), *and* questions that required fairly complex transfer ("Let's say that all the frogs get captured and taken away by hunters. What happens to the number of turtles? Does it go up, down, or stay the same?"). Thus, spaced practice improved children's ability to not only retain knowledge they learned, but also to use that knowledge in different ways.

Spaced practice benefits many types of learning, from young children learning their first concepts about the world, to medical students learning how to perform surgical operations. One study found that medical students were more successful in performing a surgery if they had practiced surgical skills in four spaced sessions that occurred once per week over four weeks, compared to four sessions that occurred on the same day.[9] For a patient undergoing surgery, the value of spaced practice cannot be overstated!

Strategies to Implement Spaced Practice

The key to implementing spaced practice is to engage students with material on multiple occasions that are separated in time. This can be done in a number of ways:

Break Up Lessons into Smaller Sessions

Instead of teaching one long lesson over a topic, divide up the lesson into smaller lessons and space them over multiple days. For example, in teaching students to conjugate verbs in a foreign language, conjugation rules can be introduced and practiced in a brief session, followed by additional practice with the same rules on subsequent days. The same goes for any academic material, such as practicing mathematical procedures, recalling terms and definitions, comparing and contrasting different concepts, or generalizing knowledge to new situations.

Revisit Concepts From Previous Lessons

It makes sense to think that once a topic has been covered, there is no need to cover it again. To the contrary, students who are learning information for the first time need to revisit it, think about it more, and process it multiple times. Such opportunities can be provided by working into class lessons some of the concepts that had been encountered in previous lessons. These can take the form of class discussions, class activities, or homework assignments that require students to retrieve previously learned information and relate it to new concepts.

Harness Technology for Spaced Study Schedules

Students can use a number of accessible online tools, such as online flashcards or calendars, to create and set a schedule with built-in reminders for studying information. With the help of learning management systems, you can also set daily quizzes designed to provide spaced retrieval practice of the concepts being learned.

Include Cumulative Retrieval Practice

Cumulative quizzes and exams facilitate spaced practice by including concepts learned at earlier points in the course. They also encourage students to study previously learned information in order to prepare for the exams. Always make sure to use spacing as a *learning* strategy throughout the semester or school year, not simply as part of high-stakes assessments.

Potential Challenges

Learning Can Feel Slow and Ineffective

When students try to retrieve information after time has passed, they will notice that they have forgotten some (or even most) of it. This could create a sense of discouragement and the feeling that they are not learning. In reality, however, information that was once learned can be re-learned more quickly with less effort, optimizing study time over time.

Spacing Can Require Some Planning

When you incorporate spacing into your classes, you might find it challenging at first to cover smaller portions of information across multiple days or to incorporate previously taught concepts into current lessons. Structuring a class to incorporate spaced practice requires some planning. Importantly, however, it does not require major restructuring or overhauls to the course, but rather a redistribution of the same amount of time that will already be spent on each lesson.

Students May Not Use Spaced Practice on Their Own

Students often opt to study information by cramming a couple of days before the exam. To encourage spaced studying, provide retrieval practice activities or brief assignments on a daily or weekly basis, rather than only one or two major exams.

Frequently Asked Questions

What is the optimal amount of spacing?

In general, the more, the better. Spaced practice is beneficial whether the lessons occur on consecutive days, one week apart, or even several weeks apart. Research shows that any spacing is better than no spacing, and exactly how much time should occur between learning sessions or the total number of sessions is less critical. You and your students should strive to space information across multiple days at long enough intervals that learning feels challenging. Importantly, these intervals can be flexible and adjusted according to your course schedule and the specific material being learned.

Should the amount of spacing stay the same or increase each time?

Research shows that the timing between sessions, whether it stays the same or increases over time, does not have a large effect on classroom learning. Students can complete two lessons with one day in-between, with five days in-between, and so on. Compared to learning the information in a single longer session, spacing benefits learning regardless of whether the time between lessons is equal or variable.

What should students do in between spaced study sessions?

Spacing benefits learning and exactly how time is spent between study sessions or lessons is less critical. For example, if students practice conjugating verbs in Spanish with spaced study sessions, they can engage in any number of activities in between, such as learning history, science, or mathematics. In fact, research has shown that alternating similar content during spaced study sessions (called *interleaving*; see Chapter 4) improves learning by providing practice at comparing and contrasting.[10] With interleaving, a student could even use the in-between time to practice conjugation in French to provide an added benefit when learning Spanish.

What should students do during spaced study sessions?

Although spacing still benefits learning even when students acquire information purely through reading or listening to a lecture, spacing is even more effective when students learn by using retrieval practice.[11] When students try to recall information, instead of just reading it, they learn it much better. In particular, repeated attempts to retrieve and review informative feedback are particularly effective for building solid long-term learning and reliable transfer of knowledge.

Further Reading

Carpenter, S. K., Cepeda, N. J., Rohrer, D., Kang, S. H. K., & Pashler, H. (2012). Using spacing to enhance diverse forms of learning: Review of recent research and implications for instruction. *Educational Psychology Review, 24,* 369–378.

Carpenter, S. K., Pan, S. C., & Butler, A. C. (2022). The science of effective learning with spacing and retrieval practice. *Nature Reviews Psychology, 1,* 496–511.

About the Author

Dr. Shana Carpenter (she/her) is a Professor of Psychology at Oregon State University near Portland, Oregon. Dr. Carpenter teaches courses and advanced seminars on introductory psychology, cognitive psychology, and research methods. She specializes in research on cognitive science principles that can be applied in classrooms to help students retain information, transfer what they have learned to new situations, and improve their awareness of their own learning. Dr. Carpenter is the author of over 70 published journal articles and book chapters, and her work has been featured in *The Washington Post, Forbes,* and *The Chronicle of Higher Education.* She earned her Ph.D. from Colorado State University.

Learn more about Dr. Carpenter at https://retrievalpractice.org/carpenter and follow her on X (formerly Twitter) at @ShanaKCarpenter.

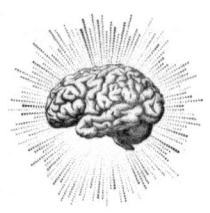

4

Interleaving

Mix Things Up to Support Long-Term Learning

Veronica X. Yan, Ph.D.

Associate Professor of Psychology,
The University of Texas at Austin

We all remember learning to identify cats and dogs as children, right? Our parents went around the neighborhood showing each dog to us and pointing them out: "dog, dog, dog, dog, dog." And then they pointed out the cats: "cat, cat, cat, cat, cat." It was a fun day. No, that didn't happen for you? Of course not — the idea of rounding up all the dogs and then all the cats is ridiculous. What is more likely to have happened is that you encountered dogs and cats throughout your life in a mixed-up order, because the world doesn't come at us one thing at a time. Rather, the world comes at us *interleaved*. Prior to starting school, we typically encounter things mixed up, but once we enter school, things start to look different.

As educators, we aim to teach our students not just so that they can regurgitate what they learn. We want them to develop conceptual understanding and skills that they can use in other parts of their lives, both in and out of the classroom. To really instill these skills with our learners, should they focus on just one thing at a time, or should they go back and forth between different concepts or skills? It turns out that researchers have studied this question in many different domains.

Let's start with an example from the sports domain, where baseball players have to learn how to swing their bats in response to different types of pitches (curveball, fast ball, changeup, and so on). In one study, researchers worked with college baseball players, assigning them to receive batting practice in one of two ways: with the pitches *blocked* by type (e.g., 15 curveballs in a row, then 15 fast balls, and then 15 changeups) or with the pitches thrown in a random, or *interleaved*, order. After six weeks of training, researchers measured how much the baseball players had improved. Those who received interleaved practice improved their hitting skills much more than those who received blocked practice (57% vs. 25% improvement).[1]

Benefits of interleaved practice have been shown for other types of motor skills (e.g., knot-tying and handwriting), for visual domains (e.g., recognizing bird species and artists' paintings styles), and for conceptual understanding (e.g., STEM and social sciences). In an experiment I conducted in high school science classrooms, I found that when difficult science concepts were interleaved on weekly practice quizzes — compared to blocked on weekly quizzes or no quizzes at all — students performed one to two letter grades higher on a final test that was administered 1–2 months after the content was initially taught.[2] Similar benefits have also been shown for many different age levels from preschool-aged children learning to adult learners (see Chapter 2 on early childhood education).[3,4]

When it comes to teaching, the beauty of interleaving is that it does not need to take more time and it does not require coming up with totally new assignments or materials; it can be as simple as re-ordering the practice questions you already assign. But, using interleaving in the most effective way does require understanding why it works so that it can be tailored to your course content and your specific students.[5]

The World Comes at You Interleaved

To make extra money in graduate school, I tutored undergraduate students in statistics. These were motivated students who dutifully completed their homework assignments. The homework assignments provided blocked practice, so all my students had to do was plug slightly different numbers into the same formula each time to get the correct answer. In preparation for the exam, they diligently memorized all the formulas and as soon as the exam started, they scribbled them out on the top of their scratch paper. But then my students would hit a roadblock. Which formula should they be using for each problem? Some students failed, not due to a lack of memorization, but due to a lack of problem-solving skills.

As I started working with these students one-on-one, I realized that this issue was linked to weak conceptual understanding and identification of the different formulas. My exam questions were interleaved, but students were so focused on just learning one formula at a time while studying that they failed to understand the similarities and differences between them.

For example, students might traditionally study concepts in a biology course one at a time: prokaryotic cells, eukaryotic cells, cell membranes, diffusion, osmosis, and active transport. But concepts and skills on exams and in real life are like a tie-dyed t-shirt: all mixed up.

How students study vs. **The exams and real life**

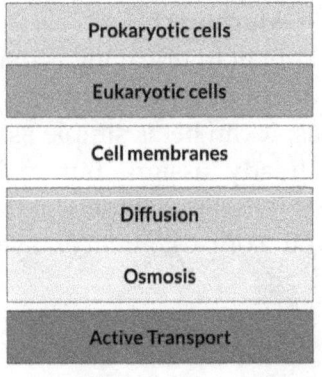
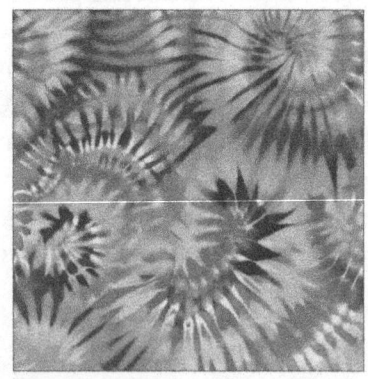

Students (and textbooks) tend to focus on just one concept or skill at a time. A review of six middle school mathematics texts commonly used in the United States found that the vast majority of math assignments use blocked practice questions; only 9.7% of the questions were interleaved in a mixed order.[6] This blocking, however, is a poor match to how concepts and skills are used on exams and in real life. Every discipline or subject area has the need for differentiation between related concepts, skills, and deeper understanding. Here are some examples:

- In English literature, interleaving helps students identify different types of storytelling structures (e.g. Freytag's pyramid, hero's journey, three-act structure, seven-point structure).

- In philosophy, interleaving helps students understand the similarities and differences between philosophical approaches.

- In cognitive psychology, interleaving helps students identify which biases and heuristics are relevant to different scenarios.

- In chemistry, interleaving helps students understand the differences between alkenes, alkanes, and alkynes.

- In music and art, interleaving similar artists helps students get a better sense of how artists differ from each other in subtle ways.

Interleaving facilitates learning to distinguish between related and confusable concepts. And going back and forth between concepts helps to build deeper conceptual understanding. When I tutored statistics, I found that juxtaposing the different formulas helped students notice that each inferential statistics test shared a similar underlying structure, and students were better able to map specific features from each formula to the scenario that called for it. And I use statistics in my everyday life as a psychology researcher to analyze data and answer research questions, but there's no set order for what statistical test I'll need to use each day. The world demands that we use skills in an interleaved manner, so we should be practicing in an interleaved manner, too.

How to Implement Interleaving

When and how to interleave concepts depends on the combination of your course content and what your students do and do not yet know. It's important to be mindful of your learning objectives and what students are having trouble with before you begin to interleave concepts. Sometimes, a concept can be complex and it may first require blocked practice for learners to get a grasp of it before they can start comparing and contrasting with other concepts.

Start with Blocking for Challenging Concepts

Think of some of the concepts in your course that students have the most difficulty with. Are there things that they tend to confuse? Which connections tend to take your students the longest to grasp? By identifying these key difficulties and common confusions, you can identify the concepts that will benefit the most from interleaved instruction and practice.[7]

For example, a music teacher might want to teach their students about Baroque, Classical, and Romantic music. Each style has wide-ranging examples that can sound very different. If students are at the point where they still need to learn the key features of each style, then it might be best to start with some blocked instruction where learners listen to varied examples within each musical style. This blocked learning helps students figure out what commonalities are shared by pieces from the same style. Once students have formed their initial impressions of each style, then you can start interleaving the different styles to ensure that students are able to notice the differences between musical styles and deepen their understanding.

In other words, there are some situations where it makes sense to start with blocked instruction and practice. Appropriate sequencing of learning relies on your teacher expertise — expertise in both the content, as well as in knowing your students. If a single concept is complex or has many different examples where students have trouble identifying the abstract principles, then start with blocked instruction and practice before jumping into interleaving.

Interleave Existing Content

Once you have identified the key concepts to deepen and strengthen, it's time to consider how to put interleaving into practice. One easy thing to do is to take existing homework or practice questions and mix them up. For newer concepts, start with blocked practice for a few questions about each concept to build familiarity and then introduce interleaved practice. But interleaving doesn't only have to look like homework or a quiz. Here are some ideas that might spark inspiration:

- **State the difference**: Draw explicit attention to contrasts and comparisons by calling back to previously taught concepts. I do this in my lectures by asking questions like, "What have we already covered in this class that this idea reminds you of?" and "What's the difference between concept A and concept B?"

- **Draw it out**: Have students make Venn diagrams or concept maps of related concepts to highlight their similarities and differences.

- **Find the connection**: Create a flashcard stack of concepts. Draw two randomly and challenge students to connect the two concepts. Make this a competition or game for more interactivity.

- **Role plays and debates**: Get students to practice applying different theories or perspectives to a scenario by asking them to take on different roles or sides (e.g., in a philosophy class, pretend to be Kant or Nietzsche).

Combine Interleaving with Longer-Term Spaced Practice

Interleaving doesn't only direct learners' attention to critical features and connections, but it can also support long-term memory through distributed or *spaced practice* (see Chapter 3). Spaced practice, or revisiting concepts over time, is baked into interleaved practice. By juxtaposing different concepts, the practice of any one concept is spaced out. This spacing supports long-term memory, so that students don't just understand it during the one lesson, but they are able to sustain that learning into the future, too. When combining interleaving and spacing, think about how your course concepts keep coming back beyond initial instruction and practice.

I teach an undergraduate course called Cognition, Human Learning, and Motivation, which meets twice a week on Tuesdays and Thursdays. I have built interleaving and spacing intentionally into my course in multiple ways:

- During interactive lectures on Tuesdays, I frequently ask students to think about how that day's content connects back to previous content. For example, when I talk about multimedia learning principles, I ask students to make connections to working memory, a concept taught the previous week.

- During group work on Thursdays, my students apply the concepts from class in an interleaved manner. In the week I teach about multimedia learning principles, I give students examples of instructional materials (e.g., a textbook page or an educational video) and they identify the multimedia principles that were present and those that were violated.

- Throughout the semester, course concepts continuously crop up in weekly cumulative quizzes, where all previously taught content is fair game. They come up more frequently at first, on each of the two subsequent quizzes, but then might not appear again for another month. The principles are built into my rubrics for future assignments where students have to design presentations or activities, as well.

My students have told me that they were skeptical about the interleaved, cumulative quizzes in my course at first, but they really appreciated it when exam weeks came around. One student said, "I realized that I had actually learned the things we covered in class. I didn't have to study and re-learn everything again right before the exam. I felt so much less stressed about your exam because of interleaving, compared to my other class exams."

Support Student Motivation

Interleaved practice can feel difficult because it requires more effort to have to go back and forth between different concepts and it can lead to more mistakes. But that's a good kind of effort and those are good kinds of mistakes to be making (see Chapter 7 about the effective teaching cycle). Interleaving reveals to students the possible confusions they might have and it gives them the type of practice that better matches final exams and real life.

However, students sometimes think that if something feels difficult, it means they are not learning,[8] so it is vitally important that you explain the purpose of interleaved practice to your students. Here are some approaches that might help your students lean into interleaved practice:

- **Meaningful alignment to real life**: Create assignments and projects that are aligned with life experience, so students flexibly draw upon different concepts and skills just like they would in the real world.

- **Keep it fresh**: Encourage your students to interleave by framing it as a positive and more interesting challenge to go back and forth between different types of questions, rather than doing the same thing over and over again.

- **Make it interactive**: Turn an interleaved quiz into a game with a leaderboard or teams.

- **Reduce anxiety**: Use smaller interleaved, cumulative quizzes to help students study effectively throughout the course instead of cramming for a final exam.

Final Thoughts

Intentionally building interleaving into your teaching and assignments can be a powerful strategy for accelerating, strengthening, and sustaining your students' learning. It supports attention to critical distinguishing features, it supports the development of fluency with skills, and it supports long-term retention. Initially, interleaving may feel more difficult, but because it supports learning in these ways, the payoff is great: better performance on high-stakes assessments, with less anxiety and more meaningful learning that can be applied in real life.

Further Reading

Sana, F., & Yan, V. X. (2022). Interleaving retrieval practice promotes science learning. *Psychological Science, 33*(5), 782–788.

Yan, V. X., Sana, F., & Carvalho, P. F. (2024). No simple solutions to complex problems: Cognitive science principles can guide but not prescribe educational decisions. *Policy Insights from the Behavioral and Brain Sciences, 11*(1), 59–66.

About the Author

Dr. Veronica Yan (she/her) is an Associate Professor of Psychology at The University of Texas at Austin in Austin, Texas. Dr. Yan teaches courses for college students, graduate students, and pre-service teachers on learning, metacognition, and self-regulated learning. Her research bridges social, cognitive, and educational psychology fields to explore how we can empower people to become motivated and effective self-regulated learners. Dr. Yan's own educational experience has spanned multiple countries, including primary and secondary school in Hong Kong, undergraduate education in England, and graduate school in California. She earned her Ph.D. from the University of California, Los Angeles.

Learn more about Dr. Yan at https://retrievalpractice.org/yan and follow her on Bluesky at @VeronicaYan.

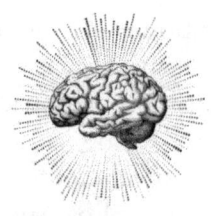

5

Metacognition

Monitoring, Control, and Trusting in the Self

Lisa K. Son, Ph.D.
Professor of Psychology, Barnard College

Consider this scenario: In school one day, your math teacher is giving a lecture on how to multiply fractions. Although you are listening carefully, you feel unsure about your level of understanding. Right on cue, the teacher calls on you to solve a problem on the board and you fail.

After class, you don't feel good — you are keenly aware that you still don't know how to multiply fractions. You consider visiting your teacher's office hours to get another chance to learn. But you don't want to "be found out" that you can't keep up, so you decide to pass on that chance and hope that you miraculously figure something out on your own.

The events in this scenario illustrate two processes that make up metacognition: *monitoring* and *control*.[1] Regardless of whether or not we know something (like how to multiply fractions), knowing that we know — or in this case, knowing that we *don't* know — can be an indication of accurate monitoring (i.e., "knowing thyself"). Subsequently, accurate monitoring allows us to have effective control of our behavior. For instance, in the opening scenario, one smart control strategy — based on your monitoring that you don't know how to multiply fractions — might have been to visit the teacher's office hours to seek help. Sometimes, however, students forego decisions that may have been ideal.

Put simply, the basic framework of metacognition includes two key components:

- **Monitoring**: the process of reflecting on your learning or knowledge

- **Control**: the process of using your self-reflections to guide subsequent behaviors

As you can imagine, in many learning contexts these two processes depend on one another: If a student's reflections are accurate, then the student has a good chance of appropriately choosing whether to seek more information.[2] If a student's reflections are flawed, they may select inappropriate strategies, hurting their chances at successful learning. Note, however, that even when a student's reflections *are* accurate, good behaviors are not guaranteed — perhaps because revealing one's lack of knowledge is easier said than done.

One fortunate aspect of metacognition is that we *all* have the ability to monitor and control our learning. Some research has shown that this ability — to reflect on your ideas about your own thinking — begins to develop at young ages. Interestingly, data show that some preliminary metacognitive processes can be expressed in non-human animals,[3] providing a strong case for an evolutionary path from a non-verbal type of metacognition to the kind of full-blown metacognition we see in humans.

Thus, metacognitive processes may not require overt language and they are typically unobservable. Take monitoring, for instance. The process of monitoring our own thoughts can be highly private, which is why metacognition has been described as a type of "internal curiosity."[4] Think of the millions of times you silently evaluated your own thoughts — when studying on your own or even when collaborating on a group project. And think about all of the self-reflections no one else knows about, not even your best friend. While it is a good thing to have private access to your own mind, you can imagine the complexities that arise for researchers who want to understand how metacognition works or for teachers who want to know how well their students are learning.

When students keep their private thoughts private, at times cutting off the control component (for example, when students don't raise their hand in class or they refuse to attend office hours), educators may believe, mistakenly, that their students have learned the material pretty well. This is not to say that students should blurt out everything they are thinking. Rather, it is important to be open about learning when it isn't going well, and to give oneself the best opportunity to seek the necessary information to fill in any knowledge gaps.

When and Why Metacognition Can Break Down

Given the potentially private nature of metacognition, successful learning may be dependent on a clearly communicated monitoring and control process between teachers and learners. Consider a scenario slightly different from the one earlier: Your teacher is giving a lesson on fractions, but rather than asking you to try solving a problem, they instead solve it for you. In other words, rather than being required to actively come up with a solution on your own, you can sit back and listen to the solution to the problem. When the teacher then asks, "You understand this, right?," you may be at risk for believing that you understand it, even when you really don't.

In this type of situation — where passive, but not active, learning occurs — monitoring is less likely to be accurate and students may *overestimate* their learning.[5] Overestimation is likely to occur when the learning strategy is too easy or too comfortable, such as when students are passive listeners or readers. On the other hand, when learning is relatively difficult, such as when students are effortfully or actively engaged with the material (what we call a *desirable difficulty*), students and teachers can get a more realistic, albeit less comfortable, view of what students do and do not know.

A breakdown in control, sadly, is also common. Even if a student knows that they don't know, it's easy to imagine them avoiding control strategies that would be ideal, such as raising their hand and asking the teacher to go over the material again. But why might these control strategies be difficult? Such control strategies might be passed over if students would rather keep their uncertainty to themselves. This behavior — of avoiding "being found out" — is a classic symptom of *impostorism*,[6] the fancier term for the layperson's "impostor syndrome." Think about the many times you have wanted to raise your hand to seek confirmation or ask a friend for help. Were there some instances where you decided not to? Could the reason have been that you felt like it would be embarrassing to be less knowledgeable than others? If so, then you may have lost an opportunity to exhibit effective control.

In the metacognitive literature, much of the research on control strategies has focused on individual skills, including time allocation, self-testing, and scheduling of study, such as spacing versus massing.[7] However, researchers have spent less time emphasizing the importance of a social control strategy that is crucial in the real world: information-seeking or *help-seeking*.[8] You can imagine a number of reasons why help-seeking may not always be popular. Maybe a student doesn't want to admit that they don't know. Maybe they're afraid that the teacher thinks they were lazy and didn't prepare for class. And maybe the student is worried that they are not qualified for the course, especially when their peers seem to know it all. These types of worries define impostorism, which refers to the feeling of being a fraud or not as good as others, despite one's objective skills.[9]

Recent data have shown that when solving difficult math problems with a "help button" that participants could click on when stuck, college students who fell higher on a scale measuring impostorism were more hesitant to click the help button than those who fell lower on the scale.[10] In other words, feeling like an impostor may inhibit a perfectly good control strategy.

To sum up some of the reasons for why students don't always exhibit good metacognition:

- Breakdowns in monitoring often occur in situations where students are passive, which doesn't allow them to assess a true lack of understanding information. Consequently, they can feel overconfident.

- Control strategies are impacted by the way students feel when they are perceived by others, especially in a social environment such as in a classroom. If students have worries that they are not qualified to be in the class — an impostor — then they might do what they can to hide any weaknesses they see in themselves. Consequently, it might be difficult to ask for help.

How Teachers Can Improve Metacognition

Given the reasons for why students' monitoring and control processes can break down, it is important to support students in the classroom. To ensure accurate monitoring, students should be given opportunities to self-reflect on their learning *during* the learning process, not just at a final test after learning is expected to be complete. At the same time, learning should not be so difficult and uncomfortable that students become discouraged and want to give up.

Here are questions that teachers can ask to encourage students to accurately monitor their learning:

Questions to Ask Before a Lesson

- Have students make confidence predictions about concepts they are learning *before* you present new information.

- Have students respond to new questions or write their own test questions a few days before a test or exam to make them more aware of their own knowledge.

Questions to Ask During a Lesson

- Rather than asking students, "Will you remember this?," ask them, "How *confident* are you that you will remember this concept next week?" This will prompt students to think about their future performance.

- Rather than asking students, "Do you understand?," ask them, "You might understand this now, but when might you forget it?" This can encourage students to think about the fact that learning is difficult and knowledge can decay.

Taken together, by asking these questions during learning, two things occur. First, monitoring is likely to be accurate given that full learning has not yet occurred. In other words, overestimation in one's knowledge is unlikely. Second, by asking these questions, students can learn that it is okay to take one's time and to be imperfect. If students know that you understand the importance of accurate reflection, then they have a better chance of learning to trust their own monitoring.

Similarly, you can play a key role in fostering a classroom filled with good metacognitive control. You can first acknowledge that learning is not easy or quick — and certainly not to be done alone. In fact, when students are quiet and passive, it may mean that they have not understood the material to a level at which they can even formulate a question. In these cases, you can help your students seek help by doing the following:

Ask Students to Record Their Thinking Strategies

Learning journals give students space to reflect on their learning. The journal could be a traditional paper journal, an online document, or even a video or audio recording. In a math journal entry, for instance, a student could write about:

- How they worked to understand a problem, including how long it took and where they were confused
- How they tried to solve the problem, including solutions that failed
- How they changed the frame or schema they were using initially and why it was challenging
- How they eventually arrived at and checked their solution, and made an assessment about the accuracy of their solution

As another example in an English literature class, students can reflect on their approach to a writing prompt, their choices for structure and syntax, and their ultimate decisions when considering feedback and making revisions.

Provide and Highlight Opportunities for Failure

One key symptom of impostorism is the fear of failure. And often, students who feel like a fraud will avoid situations when failure could occur. As a consequence, they will miss out on opportunities for feedback, and in many cases, give up entirely. Given the culture of perfectionism in today's day and age, it is important to help students know that failure is a normal and necessary ingredient for successful learning. Here are a few things you can do:

- Provide mini-quizzes that are ungraded, so that students can have an opportunity to fail safely, without worrying about their performance in the class.
- Have students discuss how long they took to learn the material and if they self-tested or used other active (as opposed to passive) techniques.

- Encourage students to take on the teacher role when possible: in study groups, by tutoring, through class participation, etc. Teaching is the best way to learn because you become aware of your gaps in understanding. In addition, group learning can be a relatively non-intimidating environment in which students can take off their impostor mask.

Model Your Own Learning Process

Regardless of what the course content is — be it history, math, or German — you should be a role model for learning. Rather than merely exhibiting your current expertise, it would be informative for you to talk about your own learning process, even if it was years (or decades!) ago. This would allow students to remember that learning is not a quick-and-easy thing, and it helps create a social environment devoid of impostors where the default may be to value natural talent over effort. Some kinds of things you can mention are things like:

- "I remember getting a very poor grade on my first history essay and some of the feedback from the teacher was unclear. I was nervous and a little embarrassed about reaching out to the teacher, but after going to office hours, I had a better understanding of how to take the reader's perspective and make my essay clearer."

- "I imagine that tonight's homework on German idioms should take about an hour. If you've worked for an hour and you're still not done, stop and let me know how much you got done." This kind of statement would allow you to know where your students' level of understanding is, as well as show students that it's okay to take their own amount of time with real effort.

- "When I was first learning about how to multiply fractions, it took me several days and several extra tutoring sessions to finally get it." This would show your students that you (the teacher) had to put in the effort to get to where you are now.

These types of statements, when made by a teacher, can be powerful in creating a shift in the learning environment. Often, when control breaks down, it's not due to a problem with the student's metacognitive thinking. Rather, the intent for choosing beneficial control strategies is there, but it's simply that students may be intimidated by a "naturally smart" teacher. Just as impostorism is contagious, good metacognition can be contagious, providing the antidote for feeling like a fraud.

Final Thoughts

- **Metacognition includes two components, each of which can break down**: *Monitoring* is a process of self-reflecting upon our knowledge. *Control* allows us to choose strategies for seeking information we don't yet have. When learning is passive, or when students feel like an impostor, they may make sub-optimal metacognitive decisions.

- **Metacognition and impostorism are, in a sense, opponents**: If students trusted their own self-reflections, then good control behaviors would be easy to exhibit. However, when students feel that they somehow got to where they are (for example, an advanced class or a selective club) despite being somewhat unqualified, they may choose to hide their uncertainties, ceasing important control behaviors such as help-seeking.

- **Metacognition can be improved through smart teaching**: By engaging students in frequent reflection on their learning progress during class, by providing opportunities for safe failure, and through role-modeling, students can gain more confidence to trust their own reflections, inspiring collaborative behavior and improving social norms.

Further Reading

Chen, S., & Son, L. K. (2024). High impostors are more hesitant to ask for help. *Behavioral Sciences, 14*(810), 1–17.

Jirout, J. J., Evans, N. S., & Son, L. K. (2024). Curiosity in children across ages and contexts. *Nature Reviews Psychology, 3*(9), 622–635.

About the Author

Dr. Lisa Son (she/her) is a Professor of Psychology at Barnard College in New York City, New York. Dr. Son teaches courses and advanced seminars on cognitive psychology and metacognition. Her research focuses on metacognition, how accurately people know the "self," and the optimization of long-term retention. Dr. Son has received funding from the U.S. Department of Education for her work with children and she has been a Fulbright Scholar to South Korea. Her books in Korean, *Metacognition* (2019) and *Impostor* (2022), have raised cross-cultural awareness of illusions during learning and biases that threaten the well-being of all individuals, including those who have achieved success. She earned her Ph.D. from Columbia University.

Learn more about Dr. Son at https://retrievalpractice.org/son and follow her on LinkedIn at https://linkedin.com/in/lisa-son-a1ba144.

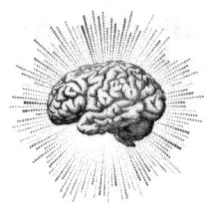

6

Concept Mapping

Strengthen Learning with Linking Words

Kripa Sundar, Ph.D.

Founder and Lead Researcher, EdTech Recharge

Growing up, I changed schools a lot, and with that came the need to navigate a wide range of school systems. By the time I was done with college, I had experienced the U.S. school system, the British school system, and two different school systems in India. Phew! What this meant for me as a learner was that I had to adapt how I studied to meet teachers' expectations in each specific situation.

Over time, I practiced a study strategy that appeared to work regardless of which school system I was in: concept mapping. Years later, I delved into the research on concept mapping and I truly appreciated it as a flexible and accessible tool for all learners. Now, as a cognitive scientist, educator, and parent, I continue to see the value of research and practice for using this learning tool.

Concept maps are graphic organizers or visual representations of knowledge, and the act of constructing concept maps is referred to as *concept mapping*. Over the years, the term "concept maps" has been used interchangeably with other phrases such as mind maps, spider maps, and idea webs, but they all follow the same basic idea: Information to be learned is presented visually in a node-link-node format to identify key concepts and their relationships. *Nodes* represent key concepts (which are usually nouns) and the nodes are *linked* by directional arrows and descriptive words that define the relationship between the nodes.

A concept map can also have a *guiding question* to frame the scope of the map and make it more manageable, similar to a title or learning objective. For example, here are two guiding questions:

- What is the relationship between driving a car and ocean acidification?

- What is the relationship between human activities and ocean acidification?

There is a subtle difference between these guiding questions: whether they ask about driving a car or human activities. A concept map for the first guiding question about driving cars could have basic nodes or concepts (e.g., fossil fuels, carbon emissions, ocean water, etc.) with action linking words (uses, dissolves in, etc.).

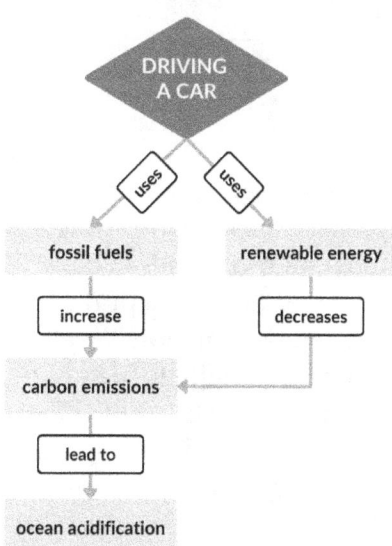

A concept map for the second guiding question about human activities would likely be more complex. The nodes might convey broader concepts (the environment, renewable energy, recycling) and the linking words could be more specific (helped by, hurt by, etc.).

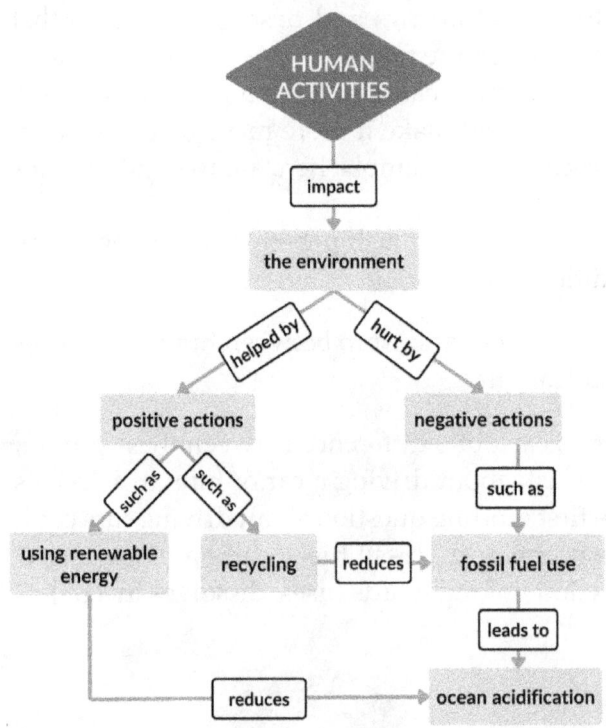

Framing the right-sized guiding question to generate key concepts on a map might take some practice. The flexibility in structure and questions can sometimes make it uncomfortable for us as educators, but remember that concept maps are intended to be a learner's visual representation of how *they* connect the concepts. Some students' concept maps might go hierarchical top-down, others could have a left-to-right approach, while a few students may see it as a cyclical map. In an era when knowing how to frame questions grows more critical, creating guiding questions can be a fun activity for your students, as well.

Why Linking Words Are Important

Here is a key question to consider: What differentiates an effective concept map from other graphic organizers, or even a paragraph or list of responses? Teachers and learners typically focus on big concepts and nodes during learning, but often expertise comes from seeing how concepts are connected with linking words. Concept mapping can be a powerful tool to help learners connect new information with prior knowledge, especially when learners carefully select linking words.[1] While learners can showcase this understanding in written text or simply with directional arrows, concept maps using linking words explicitly define the relationship, which also makes them incredible tools for studying with retrieval practice and spaced practice (see Chapters 1 and 3).

The beauty of concept maps with linking words is that it makes individual differences visible. For example, imagine two concept maps that identify the relationship between apples and pie. These two nodes can be connected in different ways for different people. One student might use the linking words "taste best in" to connect apples with pie, whereas another student might use the linking words "are a filling in" to connect apples with pie.

Which of these linking words is more effective for learning, taste or filling? The first linking word (taste) is an opinion, whereas the second linking word (filling) is a factual statement. A student's response depends on context and prior knowledge. For example, was the concept map created in response to a guiding question about the uses of apples or about a student's favorite dessert?

When your students are concept mapping, make sure they explicitly label the relationship between the two concepts they are connecting. Encourage them to use verbs and classifiers that describe the relationship in specific terms. Often, students create a concept map without linking words or they use words that describe a general relationship (the taste of apple pie) rather than a specific, explicit connection (apples are a filling in pie). In addition, the absence of linking words highlights possible confusion, gaps in understanding, or perhaps a lack of vocabulary knowledge (especially in jargon-heavy subjects). If a concept map doesn't describe the specific relationship between concepts, it will be less effective for studying and learning. What matters most is that learners connect relevant concepts with explicit linking words.

Why Concept Maps Improve Learning

The process of concept mapping reflects the *encoding-storage-retrieval model* of learning, which translates to a simplistic input-storage-output model of learning.[2] Concept mapping can be used to encode, input, learn, and organize new information in a format that helps the brain retain, retrieve, and output the required knowledge when needed. In this way, concept mapping engages multiple strategies:

- When learners describe the relationships between concepts using linking words, they practice elaboration, which improves *encoding*.

- Organizing concepts in a structure that reflects a learner's mental schema supports their *storage* of key concepts.

- When a learner generates concepts and nodes, they engage in the process of *retrieval* practice.

Multiple meta-analyses summarizing research across dozens of studies over decades consistently present evidence that learners who engage in concept mapping outperform those who may limit their learning and studying to lectures, discussions, text summaries (outlines or lists), etc. across ages, settings, and subject areas.[3,4,5] Importantly, learners who *construct* concept maps usually outperform those who only study them, further emphasizing the relationship between retrieval practice and learning.

How to Use Concept Maps in the Classroom

Concept mapping is rich and varied in its classroom applications, including formative assessments, and a method to developing critical thinking.[6,7,8] Here are three ways concept maps can be implemented in your classroom.

Expert Maps

Expert concept maps, created by the teacher, can provide snapshot summaries of key concepts and relationships within a unit. These are completed concept maps that students can reference during lessons to situate what they are learning in the bigger picture. Just remember to break the concept maps into manageable chunks to avoid "concept map shock" when a learner becomes overwhelmed with the scope and connections in the map.

For example, when I teach, I use my learning objectives as guiding questions when I create an expert map. I work through the list of concepts I *need* my learners to know and concepts I *want* my learners to know. Drawing a map of concepts related to the learning objectives and identifying how they relate with each other often forces me to recognize a possible *expertise reversal effect* where I've blended together many small topics into one concept. My first drafts of these expert maps are often scribbly, all-over the place, and truthfully overwhelming. This process forces me to prioritize the topics I cover or the relationships I can explore in the time I have. My completed expert map also signals to my students the topics we'll be covering and why.

Note-Taking

There are so many ways to use concept maps for note-taking. For instance, you can frame lesson-level guiding questions, and have students retrieve key concepts to craft their own concept maps. This approach might be more fun and insightful if students build their maps using technology, which can allow them to revisit and update their representation of the concepts, as well as reflect on how their knowledge has changed over time.

If you have very brief lessons, consider encouraging the class to keep a chart with a running list of key concepts from the beginning of the unit and have students build a concept map — individually or collaboratively — at the end of the unit. This approach gets you the bonus of visual reminders for key vocabulary, too.

This strategy is possible even with younger learners. I conducted research with a lead teacher and her class of kindergarteners to help the kindergarteners create their concept maps using pictures, arrows, and printed labels.[9] The teacher modeled the activity and then the kids paired up to work on their map about the four seasons of the year. What was so fascinating for me was that students replicated their teacher's map on their first two attempts and they made more unique connections their third time using the same pictures! This is another demonstration of how frequent retrieval practice and guided elaboration lead to successful and meaningful concept mapping.

Formative Assessments

Concept maps in almost any form (except expert maps) can serve as formative assessments. The simplest way I've seen concept maps serving as formative assessment is by having students complete partially filled maps where either the concept nodes or the relationship linking words are blank.[10] This approach lowers cognitive effort for the learner by using scaffolding. At the same time, it facilitates speedy grading since the map is a graphic fill-in-the-blank, and it facilitates structured peer discussions focused on specific relationships. You might experience some friction in the classroom when this approach becomes harder for students whose minds may have organized information differently. For this reason, partially filled concept maps might be appropriate where there are concrete and predetermined relationships between concepts (for example, speed, time, and distance in a physics course).

Trade-Offs

As much as I may love concept mapping, I'd be remiss to not point out the top two trade-offs you'll have to consider when implementing concept mapping in your classroom.

Time

Effective concept mapping takes time and practice. Good concept maps cannot be rushed since they require critical thinking. However, there are two ways to speed up the process:

First, prepare summary or expert concept maps for each unit. These concept maps can serve as your learners' "cognitive hooks" to place what they are learning and see how it all comes together. While this will still take time for you as the educator, you'll most likely be able to reuse these expert concept maps for future teaching. You could also split the workload with other teachers in your grade or department to make the expert concept maps.

Second, have your learners build a concept map soon after they learn the information. For example, ask students some simple questions as they work through the concept map: What did we know about this topic beforehand? What were some new concepts? How do they relate to what we already know? This will make the process of concept mapping quicker and easier for students.

Effort

Learning always takes effort. Building a concept map may take more effort and intellectual honesty because learners need to prioritize key concepts, recognize gaps in knowledge, and understand the organization of concepts. Often in practice, learners skip the linking words to reduce effort or they opt for the simplest/most basic relationship between concepts. Even though skipping linking words may be quicker and easier, it limits the student from using the map effectively while studying, and it limits you from getting a clear representation of learner understanding as a formative assessment tool.

You'll also need to recognize that while concept mapping may come naturally to some learners, most learners will require explicit training and practice.[11] Consider using different types of concept maps during class and gradually increase the level of cognitive effort needed. For instance, you might start with an expert map you created and then give them fill-in-the-blank maps (remove the concept or the linking words). When learners are familiar with the structure and use of concept maps, ask them to build small concept maps with targeted guiding questions before moving on to bigger and more complex questions.

Final Thoughts

As an educator, learning scientist, parent, and an immigrant for whom English isn't my first language, there are three reasons why I strongly advocate for concept mapping:

- Concept mapping is flexible in so many ways. It can be done independently, in pairs or in groups, with or without technology, using simple or complex guiding questions. In my mind, this flexibility makes concept mapping a "Swiss Army knife" in the toolkit of learning strategies.

- Concept mapping is accessible for learners of all ages and abilities. The focus on concepts and relationships reduces the burden on English language learners and those who have trouble reading and comprehending complex text.

- When a learner generates a concept map, they showcase their own learning, opening up a conversation for personalized learning. The effort a learner puts into concept mapping encourages critical thinking, reflection, and metacognition in identifying what they know, what they don't know, and how to approach additional learning.

Further Reading

Sundararajan, N. K. (2022). Concept mapping: A powerful tool for learning. *American Educator, 46*(1), 40–47.

Sundararajan, N. K., Adesope, O., & Cavagnetto, A. (2018). The process of collaborative concept mapping in kindergarten and the effect on critical thinking skills. *Journal of STEM Education, 19*(1), 5–13.

About the Author

Dr. Kripa Sundar (NarayanKripa Sundararajan, she/her) is the Founder and Lead Consultant at EdTech Recharge in Irvine, California. Her boutique impact research and consulting firm supports mission-driven education leaders to execute evidence-based product strategy toward implementation and measurement at scale, including global companies across the United States, United Kingdom, Canada, Spain, Australia, and India. Dr. Sundar is also an adjunct professor and the author of a book for children and their caregivers, entitled *How Do I Learn*. She earned her Ph.D. from Washington State University.

Learn more about Dr. Sundar at https://retrievalpractice.org/sundar and follow her on LinkedIn at https://linkedin.com/in/kripasundar.

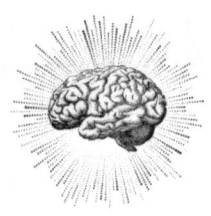

7

The Effective Teaching Cycle

Motivation, Scaffolding, and Reinforcement

Cynthia L. Nebel, Ph.D.
Director of Learning Services,
St. Louis University School of Medicine

As a first-year teacher, I remember being frustrated that so many of my students just didn't seem to care. It was so unlike how I was as a student and I found myself saying things like, "Kids these days…" Later, I stumbled upon an important realization. I always thought students needed to be motivated to learn, but there is plenty of research showing the reverse: that *learning leads to motivation*.

Students who believe in themselves and enter a learning environment open and ready to learn are more likely to succeed. We also know that success is one of the key factors that leads to higher motivation.[1,2] Once students are in the door, teachers must understand students' prior knowledge to select and *scaffold* the teaching strategies that will be most effective for learning.[3]

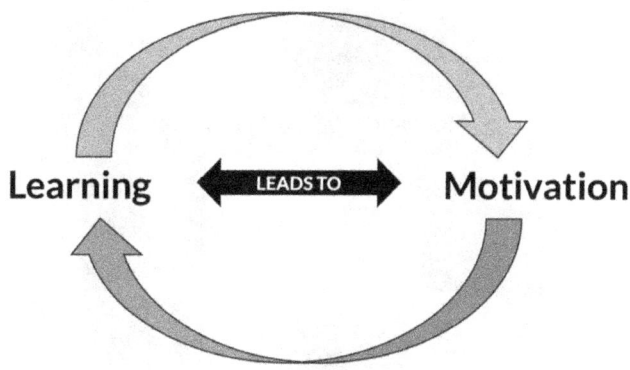

Unfortunately, many educators and students think that learning ends after the class session ends, and most teaching cycles eventually end with an assessment of student learning. But an effective teaching cycle is never "one and done." Rather, newly acquired knowledge needs *reinforcement* to be retained. Retrieval practice and spaced practice provide reinforcement, and they can be easily implemented for any age group or material that needs to be learned (see Chapters 1 and 3).[4] Because you, the effective teacher, have used appropriate scaffolding and reinforcement techniques, students are more likely to retain and succeed on assessments. This, in turn, leads to greater *self-efficacy* — students' belief in their own abilities — a key factor in motivation.

And so, we have the *effective teaching cycle* — motivation, scaffolding, and reinforcement — where each stage is critical in creating better learning for students, both now and in the future. In this chapter, I share key features of the effective teaching cycle and concrete ideas that you can use in your classroom at each stage of the cycle. There are many strategies you already use to effectively convey and scaffold material for students, and throughout this book, you'll also notice familiar strategies and new ideas for strengthening your effective teaching cycle.

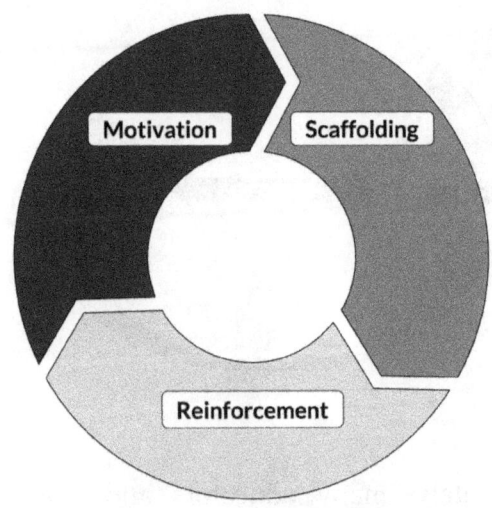

Motivation

There are many different theories of motivation, and *self-determination theory* helps identify why student motivation might be lacking. Self-determination theory explains that we have several basic needs and that, when one of these needs is not being met, motivation decreases.[5] I like to think of each of these needs as motivation "levers" that we can pull when motivation dips.

Lever 1: Perceived Value. "What's in it for me?"

Motivation increases when students recognize that what they are learning has utility and that it will be useful for them in the future (condolences to my fellow statistics instructors and all teachers who suffer at the hands of memes about learning how to play the recorder). Luckily, you can make small adjustments to your classroom approach and increase your students' perceived value of what they are learning.

Use everyday examples that students can relate to. In my statistics classes, students choose a topic they want to learn about for their final project. With my support, they design survey questions that they can use throughout the course for analyses. One student was interested in stress in student athletes and developed related questions for their survey. My students learn that statistics can have a purpose to answer questions they care about.

Talk to students about transferable skills. Sometimes they need to learn one thing so that they are better able to learn others (see Chapter 8 about transfer). And sometimes you can just remind them that getting a good grade in your class might help them get a college scholarship. And for those teaching music lessons with recorders? Some students find their passion for music right then and there, even if it's not specifically a love for a recorder. That's perceived value.

Lever 2: Autonomy. "Do I have to?"

When students perceive that they have a choice, they are more likely to be motivated to participate. No one likes being told what to do. Strategies for increasing students' autonomy include:

- A choice of topics to research for a paper
- A choice of how to demonstrate their knowledge through writing, creative projects, or a quiz
- A choice about the learning environment: where to sit, when to take breaks, etc.

Lever 3: Relationships. "Who cares whether I succeed?"

When students feel as though it matters to someone whether they succeed or fail, they are more likely to be motivated to succeed. While it is, of course, important that individual students know you care about their success, you can also foster relationships for your entire classroom:

- **Create bonds using class group work**: Encourage students to help their teammates. This may require careful cultivation of an environment where students care for one another in a way that is different from what they are used to in other classes.

- **Create space for vulnerability**: My opening ice breaker with students is for each of us to share an embarrassing memory (because I taught a course about human memory). I always went first, allowing my students to feel a bit more comfortable with one another. Later in the course, if a student answered a question incorrectly, their peers were more open to helping.

- **Use write-pair-share activities**: This gives students time to work together toward a common goal of understanding and success.

Lever 4: Self-Efficacy. "Should I even try?"

Self-efficacy refers to a students' belief in their own competency or ability to succeed.[6] Self-efficacy can be increased in a number of ways:

- **Previous experiences**: If students recognize that they have been successful in the past, they are more likely to believe that they can be successful now. This may involve offering opportunities for small wins by providing assignments that are appropriately matched to students' abilities or by directly reminding them of their past successes. For example, you could say "I know you can do this because you accomplished that other goal last week."

- **Others' experiences**: You can also describe people similar to your students who have been successful. For example, "Previous students tell me that they are worried about this assignment, but we will work through it together and you will be just as successful as the students were last year!"

- **Messages from others**: There is a benefit to simply telling students that you believe in them and in their abilities. You can also recruit parents and other students to work on boosting students' self-efficacy in this way.

- **Psychological state**: Students who are grumpy because they are tired, hungry, or just got into an argument with a friend are less likely to be motivated to learn. It's worth the time and effort to try to pump up your class and orient them to the learning environment. Some people do this through brief meditation, ice breakers, or (my personal preference) playing fun music at the beginning of class. If you notice psychological states slumping, pause and have students take a quick movement break. Breaks are useful at any age.

Scaffolding

Scaffolding, in general, refers to knowledge building upon knowledge.[7] You might start with simpler ideas (e.g., addition), and then leverage that simpler knowledge to teach something more complex (e.g., multiplication). While this is an appropriate use of scaffolding, there is another layer of scaffolding that is critical for the most effective learning to occur: You also need to scaffold *within* a domain. Consider the following example in a math class:

- Novices learn best when knowledge is given to them via direct instruction. They do best when they are shown and told how to add.

- Intermediate learners can take on more complex tasks and learn best through tasks like worked examples, where they are led through the problems they are working on.

- Relative experts (yes, a student can develop expertise in addition) learn best when they are allowed to problem-solve.

The converse of these three points is also true. Novices learn less effectively if they are thrown into problem-solving without first acquiring knowledge through direct instruction, and experts gain far less if they are explicitly taught instead of being allowed to work through problems on their own.

This idea that the best learning strategy for novices is the exact opposite for experts is called the *expertise reversal effect*.[8] It is important to have a decent understanding of how your students are progressing in their understanding of any given topic. This may mean that, in the classroom, you need to consistently assess your students in a formative way by letting them practice, so that you can see if they have mastered the material. If they are struggling to master it, then more instruction or worked examples might be needed. If they are doing well, they might be ready to move on to inquiry- or problem-based learning. This is the primary manner in which students should be differentiated in a classroom — by their learning needs, which is based on their prior knowledge and understanding of the given topic.

Reinforcement

In many classrooms, students are taught a new topic that might be assessed at a later time, but it is not always revisited in a strategic way. A key component of the effective teaching cycle is to space out review of information and to have students practice retrieving that material so that they are able to remember it in the future. You do not want your efforts to teach new material in the classroom to be wasted on forgetting, so reinforcement is a critical component of the effective teaching cycle not to be ignored.

Spaced Practice

There is a wealth of research that demonstrates that spreading out practice of new knowledge leads to much better long-term retention of that information than learning it all at once.[9] You can accomplish this in your classroom in a number of different ways. You could create a structured plan for review of content throughout the curriculum, so that you come back to material at specific points over time. One of my preferred ways of spacing review is to give students cumulative homework assignments, so that they are practicing what we're working on right now while also seeing material that we've covered in the past (see Chapter 3 for more about spaced practice).

Retrieval Practice

Spaced practice is amplified further if students are encouraged to bring information to mind. When information is brought to mind, new memory traces are laid down in the brain, increasing the strength of the memory and the likelihood of retrieving it later on. You can implement spaced retrieval practice in simple, low-stakes ways such as moving exit tickets to entrance tickets the following day or asking students questions in class about how new material relates to old material, and then having them write down answers before sharing (see Chapter 1).

Once material has been reinforced and practiced, students are more likely to be able to retrieve and use that information later on, and to feel the confidence that comes from successful retrieval.[10] That confidence will, in turn, lead to greater motivation for students, starting the cycle over and leading to even more effective learning.

Final Thoughts

You are the expert in your own classroom. Very likely, you are already engaging in many of these activities. You probably work hard to make your students know that you believe in them and that your class is important. You recognize that not every student is at the same level or ready to move on to more challenging assignments or tasks. And you probably revisit content, particularly when you feel like students didn't understand it the first time. My hope is that you will finish this chapter with renewed energy to use some of the ideas throughout this book to enhance the good work you are already doing in applying the effective teaching cycle in your classroom.

Further Reading

Abel, M., & Bäuml, K. H. T. (2020). Would you like to learn more? Retrieval practice plus feedback can increase motivation to keep on studying. *Cognition, 201,* 104316.

Sumeracki, M., Nebel, C. L., Kuepper-Tetzel, C., & Kaminske, A. N. (2023). *Ace that test: A student's guide to learning better.* Routledge.

About the Author

Dr. Cynthia Nebel (she/her) is the Director of Learning Services at St. Louis University School of Medicine in St. Louis, Missouri. She is a frequent speaker at conferences around the world for K–12 schools, universities, medical schools, Fortune 500 companies, and government organizations. Dr. Nebel is passionate about promoting dialogue between researchers and practitioners. She is also an active collaborator with *The Learning Scientists* (learningscientists.org), where she produces blog posts, podcast episodes, video content, and more. She co-authored the books *Ace That Test: A Student's Guide to Learning Better* and *Uniting Learning Science and Talent Management*. She earned her Ph.D. from Washington University in St. Louis.

Learn more about Dr. Nebel at https://retrievalpractice.org/nebel and follow her on LinkedIn at https://linkedin.com/in/cynthia-nebel.

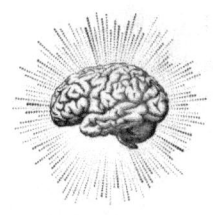

8

Transfer of Learning

Foster Students' Application of Knowledge

Steven C. Pan, Ph.D.

Assistant Professor of Psychology
National University of Singapore

Imagine that you are introducing the water cycle at the beginning of a science unit. Several days later, one of your students is walking outside. She observes a puddle that was visible in the morning, but it vanished by the afternoon. Will your student infer — drawing on knowledge from your lesson — that evaporation occurred?

Transfer of learning, or simply transfer, is the application of learned information in new situations. As educators, a fundamental goal of our instruction is that learning inside our classrooms will be applicable outside our classrooms, beyond a specific lesson, practice problem, or diploma.

How can you help students successfully apply what they have learned from one lesson to another, from one class to another, or from school to the real world? In this chapter, I share cognitive science research, practical teaching strategies, and potential challenges for enhancing transfer. With these tips, you can effectively expand your students' learning from inside the classroom to new subject areas, ideas, and real-world applications outside the classroom.

Transfer is More than Ordinary Learning

Transfer is more than the remembering of an isolated topic or concept. It involves the application of learning from an initial lesson or class to a *new* lesson or class. Cognitive scientists define transfer as extending what was learned to answer new questions, solve new problems, and facilitate new learning. In everyday life, transfer can be as simple as using information in a different way than before.

When students successfully transfer knowledge to a new situation, you often "know it when you see it:"

- An elementary school student applies their knowledge of ancient Egypt to a new lesson on ancient China
- A middle school student learns the formula for the Pythagorean theorem from an algebra class and then applies their knowledge when solving novel word problems
- A high school student writes a fiction short story and then applies their structure during literary analysis of a new story
- A college student completes a major in accounting and then applies basic accounting principles in a new job
- A medical student applies what they learn in medical school to clinical practice with patients
- An adult learner uses a flashcard app with multiple-choice questions to study for an exam with short answer questions

In each of these scenarios, if the student applies their learning in a new situation, then successful transfer has occurred. On the other hand, if earlier learning is not applied in a novel situation, then no transfer has occurred. A critical factor in these real-world examples — and in all situations involving transfer — is that learners don't simply recall information; they have to use existing knowledge in new and different ways. That's what makes transfer essential to learning.

Transfer Comes in Many Forms

Transfer is defined by two main characteristics:

- The *type* of knowledge or concept to be transferred
- A change in *context* from where learning originally took place

When the change in knowledge or context is minor, it's called *near transfer*, and when it is more substantial, it's called *far transfer*.[1] Of course, learning is complex and transfer can involve many different changes in knowledge and in context. Educators typically think of transfer of knowledge, but transfer across contexts is important, too. To give a few examples, context transfer can include a change in the physical location for learning, a change in the type of exam format, or a change in the use of the information at school or in everyday life.

	NEAR TRANSFER		FAR TRANSFER
Knowledge	Ancient Egypt in 1330 BC vs. 1325 BC	Ancient Egypt vs. Modern United States	Ancient Egypt vs. Romantic Literature
Physical	Same classroom	Different schools	School vs. everyday life
Time	In the same lesson	Weeks or months later	Years later
Task	Pythagorean calculation vs. calculation with new numbers	Pythagorean calculation vs. calculation with word problems	Pythagorean calculation vs. calculation with authentic problems
Functional	Solely academic	Academic vs. professional	Academic vs. personal
Format	Same format as before	Written vs. oral responses	Verbal vs. non-verbal

Let's go through a few examples. Do these situations involve a change in the type of knowledge, the context, or both? Are they considered to be near transfer or far transfer?

- Extending information learned about ancient Egypt to a new lesson on ancient China is a change in knowledge
- Using the Pythagorean theorem for solving novel word problems is a change in context
- Applying accounting principles in a new job is a change in context
- Switching from multiple-choice flashcards to a short answer exam is a change in context
- Applying the basic structure of short fiction when giving peer-feedback on a new nonfiction essay is a change in both knowledge and context

Of course, several changes in context can occur simultaneously. For instance, when a medical student applies what they learned in a course while treating a patient, this involves transfer across time, physical location, and function. It's important to keep in mind that whether successful transfer occurs depends on how well knowledge was learned in the first place and also the different contexts that were involved in initial learning. When taking the next step, it's important to think not just about the knowledge you want your students to transfer, but also about the different contexts that you want involved. By being mindful about shifts in context, your students' near and far transfer will be flexible, robust, and successful.

Foster Transfer with Retrieval Practice

Retrieval practice in its many forms (clickers, mini-quizzes, practice problems, and so on) is excellent for improving learning at basic and complex levels (see Chapters 1 and 2).[2] If successful transfer is the goal, then retrieval practice is definitely worth adding to your teaching toolbox. To achieve transfer, it's important to engage students in retrieval that's more extensive than standard practice questions and exercises. Here are three strategies to foster transfer using retrieval practice:

Implement Broad Retrieval Exercises

Have students retrieve not just one or two details from a lesson, but as much as they can possibly remember. Ask your students to write down everything they have learned from a lesson or everything they know about a specific topic (for example, you could ask, "Retrieve everything you know about the first stage of mitosis"). Because asking students to retrieve broadly encourages them to think about multiple aspects of the material to be learned, transfer increases. Keep in mind that with broad questions, students may need a hint or suggestion to connect prior learning in a new context.

Encourage Elaboration

Ask students to construct meaningful explanations with elaboration (see Chapter 9). This method involves more than retrieving what they have learned; it encourages thinking about the *why* and *how* of material to be learned. As a simple example, a science teacher could ask students to explain how lightning works. When students create coherent, logical explanations of a concept or topic, it improves their overall understanding and transfer.[3]

Mix Question Complexity and Format

Use a variety of questions for retrieval practice (lower and higher order, factual and conceptual, multiple-choice and short answer, etc.) to engage students in thinking about subject matter in different ways.[4,5] For example, you can scaffold a variety of questions that ask students to retrieve basic concepts, apply that information, *and* make an inference.

Feedback is the Key to Transfer

To effectively foster transfer, retrieval practice should be combined with feedback. You probably already do this with feedback clarifying misunderstandings during class or facilitating class discussion. Feedback not only helps students strengthen the knowledge that they already have; it also helps them fill in gaps in their knowledge. With feedback, your students will be better able to integrate what they have retrieved with the rest of the materials to be learned. Here are two strategies for effective feedback:

Provide Explanatory Feedback

Feedback that includes a thorough explanation of the correct answer promotes transfer.[6] Explanatory feedback should directly connect the correct answer with related concepts. Students should learn whether they retrieved the answer correctly and *why* the answer was correct. If feedback contains information beyond what was learned initially, such as novel concepts or examples, then students can build additional connections in their understanding.

Give Students Time to Process Feedback

Students have to actively engage in processing feedback in order to reap its benefits. Ideally, feedback should be self-paced without time limits. This gives students the chance to fully process the information being presented without being prematurely interrupted. In addition to time, effective processing of feedback takes energy and attention. It is sometimes easy to lose focus when it comes to learning from feedback. To improve student engagement, consider alternating back and forth between periods of retrieval practice and feedback, with breaks in between. This helps keep students "on their toes" as they retrieve and strengthen their learning.

Transfer of Learning Isn't Easy

Transfer is a fundamental "holy grail" of education. Successful transfer means that a high degree of understanding and flexible learning has been achieved. At the same time, transfer can be difficult to generate. You've probably had the experience where students may not remember what they learned from chapter to chapter, class to class, and especially not year to year. Even more frustrating, your students may remember knowledge, but it remains "inert" — they struggle to identify when it's appropriate to apply what they know. In fact, in over a century of research, cognitive scientists have discovered that successful transfer is far more challenging than you might expect.

A Classic Case of Elusive Transfer

In a famous study from the 1980s, students read a story about a military general seeking to capture a fortress that was located at the center of a country.[7] The problem in the story was that a large group of soldiers could not travel on only one road. The solution was that the soldiers had to travel in small groups, each taking a different road to reach the fortress.

After students in the research study finished reading about the fortress problem, they were asked to solve a new problem involving a physician attempting to irradiate a tumor. The problem was that a dose of radiation strong enough to destroy the tumor would severely damage nearby tissues if it was delivered all at once.

The solution to the radiology problem seems obvious: apply what was learned in the fortress problem by using smaller multiple rays. However, 43% of students failed to transfer what they had learned; they were unable to apply the simple solution from the fortress problem to solve the radiation problem.

Why Transfer of Learning is Challenging

Successful transfer is difficult to foster due to three major obstacles:

- Learners may not recognize that the knowledge they've acquired should be applied to a novel situation. This is especially the case when the transfer situation is highly dissimilar to the context in which the original learning took place. Differences in location, specific details, and how information should be used may cause learners to think that they are facing an entirely unfamiliar situation.

- Learners may recognize that they need to apply their knowledge, but they have trouble remembering the knowledge to be transferred. If they can't remember it, then they can't transfer it.

- Learners may attempt to apply their knowledge, but they do so inaccurately. In this case, although the first two obstacles have been overcome, transfer still fails to occur because knowledge has been applied in the wrong way. For example, a medical student that is treating a patient with a headache may correctly recall the relevant neurological concepts, but they could still select the wrong neurological treatment to apply.[8]

A Simple Hint Makes a Big Difference

In the study involving the fortress and radiation problems, students needed to accomplish the following:

- Remember the solution to the fortress problem

- Recognize that the fortress solution can be applied to the radiation problem

- Correctly apply the fortress solution to the radiation problem

When students were given a helpful hint that one of the stories they had read could be helpful in solving the radiation problem, nearly all of the students generated the correct solution. In this case, students' difficulty in transferring their knowledge was resolved with a simple reminder. In your classroom, offer hints or prompts to ensure students recognize opportunities to transfer their learning. You can also empower students to foster their own transfer of learning independently: acknowledge that transfer is hard, that they should take time to fully process feedback, and to recognize when prior knowledge can be applied in new contexts.

Further Reading

McDaniel, M. A., Thomas, R. C., Agarwal, P. K., McDermott, K. B., & Roediger, H. L. (2013). Quizzing in middle-school science: Successful transfer performance on classroom exams. *Applied Cognitive Psychology, 27*, 360–372.

Pan, S. C., & Rickard, T. C. (2018). Transfer of test-enhanced learning: Meta-analytic review and synthesis. *Psychological Bulletin, 144*(7), 710–756.

About the Author

Dr. Steven Pan (he/him) is an Assistant Professor of Psychology at the National University of Singapore in Singapore. Dr. Pan teaches courses on cognitive psychology and research methods. His research centers on understanding and enhancing human learning and memory, with a specific aim of developing learning strategies that yield durable and adaptable knowledge. Dr. Pan's work particularly emphasizes evidence-based approaches such as pre-testing, retrieval practice, and interleaving. He earned his Ph.D. from the University of California, San Diego.

Learn more about Dr. Pan at https://retrievalpractice.org/pan and follow him on LinkedIn at https://linkedin.com/in/steven-pan-phd-82247b1ba.

9

Bringing It Together

Bite-Sized Adjustments for Powerful Engagement

Michelle L. Rivers, Ph.D.
Assistant Professor of Psychology, Santa Clara University

Try this simple task that was mentioned in Chapter 1: Draw the Apple logo from memory. It's a familiar symbol we see nearly every day (especially where I teach in the heart of Silicon Valley in California) and yet you might be surprised at how difficult it is to get the details right (e.g., what side of the apple contains the bite?). A 2015 study found that only 1 in 85 participants could accurately recall the Apple logo, and fewer than half could identify it from a set of options.[1] This task highlights an important truth about learning: Repeated exposure to information doesn't create strong, lasting memories. In fact, passive study methods like re-reading or reviewing notes can foster overconfidence, where students believe they've mastered material they only superficially remember.[2]

How can you help your students develop deeper, more durable learning while avoiding the trap of overconfidence? In this chapter, I share five research-backed strategies that I've found effective, which address these challenges and strengthen everyday teaching routines. Each strategy is designed to be simple to implement. Instead of requiring a complete overhaul of your teaching, these small but powerful adjustments can increase engagement, deepen understanding, and foster sustainable improvements without additional lesson preparation.

Use Name Tags as Memorable Exit Tickets

What you're already doing: Using name tags to learn students' names and to help take attendance

How to make name tags more effective: Use name tents with a retrieval practice question on the inside

In my college classroom, instead of name tags, I use *name tents* that include student names, pronouns (if they wish to share), and a fun fact about themselves. I give each student a piece of cardstock or heavy paper with markers or pens. They fold the paper in half lengthwise to form a tent shape and write their name clearly in a color that's easy to read from a distance. My students place these on their desks for the first few days or weeks of class to help everyone learn each other's names.

To make name tents memorable for you and your students, reserve space inside the tent for a brief exit ticket at the end of each class to check for understanding, gather feedback, and encourage reflection. Sample exit ticket questions include: "What is one thing you learned today?," "What was the most challenging part of today's lesson?," and "How would you use what you learned today outside of class?" Ask just one question and give students 2–3 minutes to write their response inside the name tent. Collect these as students leave to help you monitor attendance, identify areas of misunderstanding, and plan future lessons.

Ask Students to Answer a "Question Du Jour" Before a Lesson

What you're already doing: Presenting students with learning objectives before diving into the topic

How to make learning objectives more effective: Present the learning objectives as questions students answer before a lesson

In my cognitive psychology course, I want students to learn the differences between short-term (or working) memory and long-term memory, and how encoding and retrieval help us retain information. Instead of introducing this learning objective as a statement with unfamiliar terms, I ask a big-picture question of the day (or a *Question Du Jour*). For example, "Why do we remember some things for a long time but forget others quickly?" I then invite students to think about this question by writing a short reflection or by discussing it with classmates to foster curiosity.

At the end of the lesson, I ask them to answer the question again, usually as an exit ticket. Comparing answers from the beginning and end of class helps my students see how much they've learned. This approach is particularly effective for topics where students often have misconceptions, as it allows them to see how their understanding has changed from the beginning to the end of the lesson.

Research on learning supports this approach, too. A study with college students found that providing learning objectives before reading a neuroscience passage helped them do better on a test, compared to when no objectives were given in advance.[3] When these learning objectives were presented as questions, students learned even more effectively than when the objectives were given as statements. Interestingly, it made no difference whether the pre-reading learning objective questions were in multiple-choice or short answer format.

You're probably used to creating learning objectives for your classes. Try rephrasing your objectives as questions that students can think about or answer before the lesson. Don't worry if students answer these questions incorrectly at first. As long as the lesson provides them with the correct information, students' initial answers can be helpful. Activating students' prior knowledge, even if it's wrong or incomplete, allows them to connect new material to what they already know. Later on, they might remember, "Oh, I used to think that was true!" and they can use their initial response as a cue to recall the correct answer after a lesson.

Add Confidence Ratings and Peer Instruction

What you're already doing: Using various forms of retrieval practice in the classroom

How to make retrieval practice more effective: Have your students rate their confidence before, during, and/or after answering retrieval practice questions, followed by discussing their answers with peers

As a cognitive scientist, I incorporate frequent low- or no-stakes retrieval practice into my classroom activities. This takes various forms: answering questions on Kahoot, playing trivia games on white boards, and completing scavenger hunt-style worksheets. One of my favorite on-the-spot retrieval techniques is to ask students a question, give them two or more response options, and have them indicate their answers by holding up their fingers. For example, in a statistics class, I might ask, "If a dataset has an outlier, which measure of central tendency is more likely to be affected? Hold up one finger if you think it's the mean and two fingers if you think it's the median." This is a quick, inclusive way to check understanding that's easy for students to participate in, especially in subjects where some students may hesitate to answer aloud.

To help students become more reflective learners and to engage their metacognition (see Chapter 5), you can also ask them to *rate their confidence* in their answers by holding up their fingers. For example, I'll say, "How confident are you that your response is correct? Hold up one finger if you're not confident (just guessing) and five fingers if you're very confident." This quick self-assessment allows students to recognize when they may need more practice or review, which also gives you insight into their grasp of the concept.

If you notice varied responses or mismatched confidence levels among your students, take this further with peer instruction. When students have different answers, prompt them to pair up and discuss their reasoning. For instance, have them find someone with a *different* answer, and then let them talk it over for a few minutes. This exercise encourages students to explain their thinking, challenge misconceptions, and learn from each other. Once they've discussed, ask them to answer the question and rate their confidence again.

Research shows that peer instruction often leads students to change incorrect answers to correct ones, even with challenging questions, and they don't simply defer to the more confident student.[4] To maximize these benefits from confidence ratings and peer instruction, follow up the activity with a quick review to clarify any lingering questions and reinforce key concepts.

Have Students Explain Their Answers

What you're already doing: Assessing student learning with multiple-choice questions

How to make assessments more effective: Invite (or require) students to explain their answers to multiple-choice questions

Multiple-choice questions are an efficient way to assess students, but answers can often be guessed correctly by chance. To make multiple-choice questions more meaningful and engaging, try having students explain their answers. This can help them think more deeply and connect what they're learning to other concepts.

In my classes, students answer multiple-choice test questions for easy grading, and I also encourage them to write a short explanation beside each question on their test. Writing explanations helps students think more critically about their answers and strengthens their understanding. When they connect new ideas to what they already know, find links between concepts, or come up with examples, they build stronger mental connections. Explaining answers also makes students more aware of what they know and don't know, which helps them become better learners over time.[5]

When students are torn between two answers, explaining their choice can often help them make a decision. Rather than just guessing, they'll search their memory for more details to support their answer. To encourage thoughtful answers, I let students earn partial credit for their explanations:

- Full credit if they choose the correct answer and give a good explanation

- Partial credit if they choose the wrong answer, but they demonstrate a strong understanding in their explanation

- Partial credit if they choose the correct answer, but they provide a weak explanation

- No credit if both the answer and the explanation are incorrect

To try this approach in your own assessments, use multiple-choice questions that prompt students to apply, analyze, or transfer concepts so that their explanations go beyond simple justifications (see Chapter 8). Allow your students sufficient time to write their explanations, especially if they're new to the process.

If grading all of their explanations feels overwhelming, consider setting a limit on how many explanations students need to provide. This approach allows them to focus on the questions they're least confident about. Finally, introduce this method gradually, such as during practice quizzes, so that students get comfortable explaining their thinking.

Teach Students How to Learn

What you're already doing: Teaching students course content

How to make learning more robust: Teach students how learning works, both inside and outside your classroom

Most students are taught *what* to learn, but they rarely receive explicit instruction on *how* to learn.[6] When I tutored K–12 students, much of my support centered on essential study skills like goal setting, time management, and active learning techniques — all foundational tools that often go untaught without direct supervision. Recognizing the importance of these skills, I now dedicate a full class session to discussing and practicing effective learning strategies with my students. Here's what this looks like in my classroom and how you can implement it in your classroom:

Ask Students About Their Study Strategies

Ask your students to share their study strategies for exam preparation and their beliefs about effective learning. This discussion often reveals that students use a mix of strategies, some of which are more effective — like retrieval practice — and others less so, such as re-reading or re-writing notes.[7] Encouraging students to share these beliefs and practices allows you to address common misconceptions about how learning works, such as "the more time you spend studying, the more you'll learn" or that "long-lasting memories are created by repeated exposure to information." Like Dr. Janell Blunt's class (see Chapter 1), I also have my students draw the Apple logo from memory to help them understand the difference between mere exposure and deeper learning.

Provide an Overview of How Our Memory System Works

Imagine you've set a specific fitness goal: increasing your bench press to 200 pounds in 12 weeks. Achieving this goal requires more than just motivation to show up at the gym. You also need to understand how your body works and how to use the equipment effectively to see consistent progress. Learning works the same way; motivation alone isn't enough. To truly improve learning, students need a basic understanding of how the human memory system functions and how to use available tools and resources effectively. Much like time spent in the gym, effective learning demands effort and commitment. After all, "No pain, no gain!" (Credit to Dr. Veronica Yan, author of Chapter 4 on interleaving, for this powerful analogy for learning.)

When I give an overview of how our memory system works, I emphasize the importance of creating strong associations between different pieces of information. I also explain the distinction between material being *available* (stored in our memory) versus material being *accessible* (our ability to retrieve that information when we need it). I aim to provide a clear framework for understanding when and why certain learning strategies are effective. I want my students to realize that the mental processes involved in these strategies matter more than the strategies themselves. For instance, many students use flashcards to study, but if they test themselves right after reviewing their notes when the material is still fresh on their mind, or they simply flip the flashcard over to see the answer without engaging in active retrieval, they miss out on the full benefits of this technique.

Model and Demonstrate Effective Learning Strategies

With a foundational understanding of the human memory system, your students will be ready to learn about specific study strategies and how to apply them. But what types of strategies should you teach them?

Self-explanation is one study strategy to help form meaningful connections, particularly when the information is relevant to everyday life. While studying, students can ask themselves *why* something is true and how it connects to what they already know. To demonstrate the power of self-explanation, I have my students learn a series of sentences (e.g., "The hungry man got into the car"). They learn one set of sentences using a rote repetition strategy (mentally repeating each sentence) and a second set of sentences using a self-explanation strategy (finding connections between the actions and characteristics of the person in each sentence). I test them on both sets of sentences and I have them compare their memory performance for each strategy.

Consistent with research on self-explanation, my students remember sentences better when they created connections while learning. After this demonstration, we discuss how to incorporate self-explanation into study routines by generating explanations for steps in a process, asking themselves why a concept might be true, or coming up with real-world examples of course material. In your classroom, model for students how they can apply the self-explanation strategy independently by asking "How does this information relate to what you already know?" after reading each section of a textbook chapter.[8]

Lecturing about the effectiveness of various study strategies might convince your students that the strategy works generally, but how do you convince them that it will work for them specifically? A crucial component is teaching students how to apply the strategies to their learning of the specific material in your course.[9] In my classroom, the strategies I emphasize vary depending on what students are learning and what study strategies they already report using. I always cover retrieval practice and spacing, as these techniques benefit all types of content (see Chapters 1 and 3).

Other study strategies I share with my students are tailored to my course content. For instance, when I worked with a general chemistry course, I taught students about *interleaving*, a learning strategy to mix up different problems or topics within a single lesson or study session (see Chapter 4). In the chemistry course, students needed to distinguish between similar concepts (e.g., identifying whether a compound is ionic, molecular, or acidic). Interleaving is especially effective for this type of learning, helping students practice the skill of differentiating among closely related vocabulary words or types of information.

Have Students Commit to Learning Goals and Develop a Plan

After discussing and practicing effective strategies, I have students set a specific learning goal for the following week (e.g., master net-ionic equations). I tell students to take out their planners or calendar apps and make a study schedule for the week. I encourage students to consider the time(s) and place(s) they will study, the concepts they will focus on, the strategies they will use, and how they will track their progress. As a class, we discuss common obstacles to studying (e.g., procrastinating, getting distracted, etc.) and strategies for overcoming them.

Throughout the term, consistently reinforce effective strategies, learning goals, and study plans. At the end of your lecture slides, include a study guide that features key terms and retrieval practice questions. Also, remind students how to effectively use these strategies to aid in their exam preparation. After each exam, facilitate an exam wrapper activity where students reflect on their learning goals and study strategies. This structured reflection promotes self-assessment, encourages students to take ownership of their learning, and fosters an empowering learning environment for you and your students.

Further Reading

Rivers, M. L. (2021). Metacognition about practice testing: A review of learners' beliefs, monitoring, and control of test-enhanced learning. *Educational Psychology Review, 33*, 823–862.

Rivers, M. L. (2023). Test experience, direct instruction, and their combination promote accurate beliefs about the testing effect. *Journal of Intelligence, 11*(7), 147.

About the Author

Dr. Michelle Rivers (she/they) is an Assistant Professor of Psychology at Santa Clara University near San Jose, California. Dr. Rivers teaches courses on cognitive psychology and research methods. They have also taught hands-on STEM topics to elementary students and tutored K–12 students. Dr. Rivers specializes in research on effective learning strategies, metacognition, and STEM learning, and they are passionate about science communication. They founded the blog *Cogbites* (bite-sized cognition, cogbites.org), where early-career scientists work together to translate research about the study of mental processes for the general public. They earned their Ph.D. from Kent State University.

Learn more about Dr. Rivers at https://retrievalpractice.org/rivers and follow them on LinkedIn at https://linkedin.com/in/mlrivers3.

10

Neuromyths Debunked

Why They Persist and How to Think Smarter

Roberta Ekuni, Ph.D.
Adjunct Professor of Psychology,
Universidade Estadual de Londrina

Have you ever heard that teaching students according to their learning style (e.g., auditory, visual, kinesthetic, etc.) can optimize their learning? Or that when children listen to classical music, it increases their intelligence and reasoning abilities? Too good to be true, right? Yes!

These misconceptions about brain functioning and learning are called *neuromyths*. Neuromyths often involve oversimplifications of neuroscience research that lead to misunderstandings about how the brain works. They can also arise from generalizations of research findings from animals, which are then incorrectly applied to humans. Two additional neuromyths include the belief that we use only 10% of our brain, and that creative people use their right brain hemisphere more, while logical people use their left brain hemisphere more.

As educators, it's important to be aware of neuromyths, where they come from, how to spot them, and how to avoid them. Classroom time and resources are valuable, and they should be allocated to effective teaching and studying, not spent on ineffective methods based on neuromyths that can ultimately hinder students' learning.

How Educators Learn Neuromyths

How prevalent are neuromyths in education? Surveys conducted around the world show that people, particularly teachers, tend to believe misconceptions about the brain.[1] It's hard to determine which neuromyths are the most widely believed, as surveys conducted in the same country yield different results. The prevalence of belief in neuromyths may depend on factors such as the survey sample, local culture, and teacher training programs.

For instance, two studies identified different "top three" neuromyths, despite both samples consisting of educators in the United States. In one study, educators largely believed in benefits from exercises to "integrate" the right and left brain, brain training games for reading and language skills, and aligning teaching with a student's predominant learning style.[2] In the other survey, researchers found the top three most-endorsed neuromyths were believing in benefits from enriched environments to stimulate brain development in preschool children, brain integration exercises, and believing sugary foods and drinks cause inattention in children.[3]

Considering the potential negative consequences of believing in neuromyths, understanding where people learn neuromyths could help to prevent their spreading. First, research shows that news and the media are sources that spread neuromyths — perhaps not intentionally, but media tends to be sensationalist by presenting information as relevant (even when it is not) and by omitting important research details.[4]

Second, we believe information when we trust the source, and we tend to trust sources that we encounter repeatedly, such as on social media. Cognitive psychology research on the *availability bias* demonstrates that when information is more familiar, people think, "I heard that before, so it must be true!" without even realizing it.

Third, teachers learn various neuromyths in their pre-service training courses and professional development programs.[5, 6] Teachers should learn accurate information in these courses; however, analyses of teacher training materials show that they contain little or no evidence-based content on effective learning strategies, such as retrieval practice and spaced practice.[7]

The Seductive Allure Effect

Neuromyths are appealing. Even the presence of the word "brain" can influence teachers' perceptions. In one research study I conducted, teachers and students read about a hypothetical educational product.[8] For one group, the product name was "Right *Start* Training." For the other group, the product name was "Right *Brain* Training." In addition, the product description included images with or without a brain. For the group of participants who saw a brain image, it was a fake MRI brain image, which had no actual connection with the product. It is worth mentioning that, for all four groups, the description about the hypothetical product was the same — only the title of the product and the presence of the brain picture changed.

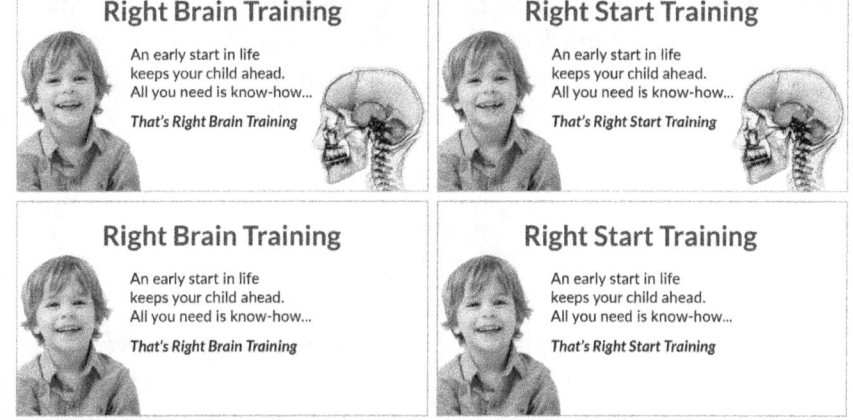

We found that teachers, compared to students, ranked the product with the word "brain" included as having more efficacy and scientific merit than the product without the word "brain" in the title. This appeal is known as the *seductive allure effect*, that is, a fascination by the brain and a hunger for brain-related information.

Similarly, it is common to see the presence of the prefix "neuro" on products and books. For instance, consider various neurodrinks and neuroeducation programs. By the mere presence of the word "neuro," these offerings become more attractive, and consequently, more people become trust them and buy them.

Surveys show that teachers report using their beliefs about the brain in their decision making. Teachers who believe in a certain neuromyth may seek "evidence" to support their beliefs, which scientists refer to as *confirmation bias*. Teachers are more likely than students to rely on intuitive or anecdotal evidence, rather than on rational or scientific sources to support their level of agreement with false statements in neuromyth surveys.[9] Since correcting one's beliefs about misinformation involves complex cognitive processes, we must avoid acquiring and spreading these inaccuracies in the first place.

While we need more data to determine how beliefs in neuromyths affect educational practices, there is concern that these misconceptions can lead educators to make harmful decisions. Since classroom time is limited, if a teacher spends their teaching time using a neuromyth, such as trying to teach according to students' learning style preferences, they may not utilize effective, efficient evidence-based techniques during that time, such as retrieval practice, spaced practice, or interleaving (see Chapters 1, 3, and 4). Therefore, using one ineffective strategy may prevent educators from employing an effective one that could improve student learning, which is an unfortunate waste of resources.

Tips to Combat Neuromyths

Due to the problems that neuromyths may cause, we need to fight against them. The first step in combating neuromyths is knowing how to identify them. Because of the seductive allure of neuroscience (also called *neurophilia*), if someone uses brain pictures or mentions neurotransmitters (e.g., dopamine) in an attempt to convince you that something is research-based, pay extra attention. Be cautious if someone is trying to sell a product or a professional development course claiming to be based on neuroscience research and ask for more information before deciding whether to invest your time and money in it.

Be skeptical of those who use authority to reinforce their claim. For example, you may hear someone state, "A professor from a prestigious university said that." Do not be surprised if the professor did not actually say that claim (or even that the so-called "professor" may not exist). So, look for information from peer-reviewed journals and be cautious with information that lacks scientific content. Think like a detective and search for the original source. For instance, if someone says, "A study shows that…," ask for the original research or try to find it yourself. If it sounds too good to be true or too generic, there is a high probability it contains inaccuracies. Question yourself and think about whether a news article is hype that takes advantage of the seductive allure effect, or whether it is based on actual science.

The lack of scientific literacy among the general population is one of the factors that makes everyone vulnerable. Practice scientific thinking and familiarize yourself with the characteristics of scientific research. You don't need to be an expert, but understanding the basics of research methods will empower you to protect yourself from neuromyths. Remember that all research has nuances and limitations. In the conclusion section of most research articles, you will find crucial information about the strengths and limitations of the paper. Here are some additional questions to consider when learning about brain research: Was the research conducted on humans or animals? Was it conducted in a laboratory or in real classroom environments? Were the materials used in the study relevant to education?

Another method for combating neuromyths is to disseminate *correct* information. Although social networks can be a source of spreading misinformation, they can also be utilized by scientific and educational communities to disseminate accurate information, with the opportunity to reach millions of people. For instance, I was invited to a podcast to talk about how to study effectively it has over 1 million views on YouTube. Also, I share information about cognitive psychology research on my Instagram account and people thank me for helping them learn how to study. I am so grateful for that!

Lastly, in addition to recognizing the quality of information, it is also important to strengthen the dissemination of evidence-based teaching and study strategies. One suggestion is to form a study group in your school with colleagues to discuss the evidence-based strategies shared in this book, especially those with real classroom applications. One resource you can also share in your study group is a neuromyths quiz in the book *Powerful Teaching*.[10] In your study group, discuss each statement on the quiz and research more about each topic together to foster collaborative critical thinking in your community.

- **Identify neuromyths**: Pay attention to claims that include terms like "neuro" or "brain." Think about whether the claim is scientifically valid.

- **Critically evaluate and investigate claims**: If someone is trying to sell a product or book, request more details before investing your time or money.

- **Be skeptical of perceived authority**: Just because an authority figure said something doesn't make the statement true.

- **Practice scientific thinking**: Spend some time studying basic research methods to protect yourself from misinformation and read the conclusion section of research articles for limitations that the scientists have identified in their own research.

- **Seek original sources**: Don't trust claims about a product where "a study shows" it works. Instead, ask, "What study?"

- **Disseminate accurate information**: Remember, the more you see information, the more likely you are to believe it. So, use your social networks to share accurate scientific information. Avoid sharing information that you are not sure is true.

- **Study with your colleagues**: Discuss and explore evidence-based teaching strategies, complete a neuromyths quiz, and foster collaborative thinking.

Final Thoughts

We are inclined to bridge neuroscience and education to improve educational outcomes. However, teachers may feel an urgency to implement neuroscience findings in the classroom. This makes them easy targets for neuromyth-based programs, creating a vicious cycle where educators end up spreading false information.

Unfortunately, there is little consensus on how to reduce or prevent beliefs in neuromyths. Some studies show that more knowledge protects teachers from neuromyths, while other studies contradict these findings.[11] Furthermore, without training in the scientific method, it can be a challenge to identify neuromyths in products, news articles, social media, and professional development programs.

Neuromyths are erroneous pieces of information surrounding the science of the brain and how people learn. There is a high level of belief in these misconceptions, especially in the educational field, which can lead educators to adopt strategies that are potentially doomed to failure. As educators become more discerning consumers of information, they will be better equipped to implement strategies that truly benefit student learning, such as retrieval practice, spacing, and interleaving. By questioning dubious claims, you can break the cycle of spreading neuromyths and create a more robust educational framework that prioritizes evidence-based techniques.

Further Reading

Luiz, I., Lindell, A. K., & Ekuni, R. (2020). Neurophilia is stronger for educators than students in Brazil. *Trends in Neuroscience and Education, 20*, Article 100136.

Sazaka, L. S. R., Hermida, M. J., & Ekuni, R. (2024). Where did pre-service teachers, teachers, and the general public learn neuromyths? Insights to support teacher training. *Trends in Neuroscience and Education, 36*, Article 100235.

About the Author

Dr. Roberta Ekuni (she/her) is an Adjunct Professor at Universidade Estadual de Londrina in Paraná, Brazil. Dr. Ekuni teaches courses on neuroscience and research methods. She specializes in research on retrieval practice, neuromyths, and cross-cultural learning. Her popular blog, videos, online courses, and articles reach thousands of students and teachers in Brazil and around the world. She earned her Ph.D. from the Universidade Federal de São Paulo.

Learn more about Dr. Ekuni at https://retrievalpractice.org/ekuni and follow her on Instagram at @DraRobertaEkuni.

About the Editor

Pooja K. Agarwal, Ph.D. (she/her) is a cognitive scientist, conducting research on how students learn since 2005. She is the lead author of the book *Powerful Teaching: Unleash the Science of Learning* and an Associate Professor at the Berklee College of Music in Boston, teaching psychological science to exceptional undergraduate musicians.

Dr. Agarwal's award-winning research has been published in prominent peer-reviewed academic journals; recognized by the National Science Foundation and the U.S. Department of Education; and featured in *The New York Times*, *Education Week*, *Scientific American*, and *NPR*.

Drawing on her combined 20 years of experience as a scientist, public school teacher, and college professor, Dr. Agarwal shares practical research-based resources for thousands of educators around the world at *RetrievalPractice.org*. Her love of learning formed at the outset of her career as a 4th and 5th grade teacher, and she earned her Ph.D. from Washington University in St. Louis.

Learn more about Dr. Agarwal at https://retrievalpractice.org and follow her on various social media platforms at @RetrieveLearn.

Acknowledgments

As editor, I would like to thank the authors who contributed to this book: Janell Blunt, Shana Carpenter, Roberta Ekuni, Lisa Fazio, Cindy Nebel, Steven Pan, Michelle Rivers, Lisa Son, Kripa Sundar, and Veronica Yan. This book feels like a family reunion (I should get us matching t-shirts). We've conducted research and published together, spent time at awkward conference happy hours together, and talked about teaching and research late into the night together. We've swapped dog photos, supported each other during hard times, and celebrated our accomplishments during happy times. Thank you for generously sharing your ideas and research with the world.

I would also like to thank my teaching friends, writing friends, and best friends who continue to provide me with inspiration, advice, and a listening ear: my mother Anu, Geoff Maddox, Ludmila Nunes, Chuck Rickert, Peter McIntyre, Jen Duclose, Marti Epstein, Marcela Castillo-Rama, Erica Knowles, Alicia Bower, Michael Heyman, Patrice Bain, Shelly Mrozek, Matt Miller, Julie Maurer, Susan Randall, Alexandra Schweitzer, Angela Gallagher, Megan Bishop, Kate Gagnon, Liz Albro, Roddy Roediger, Ayanna Thomas, Marianne Lloyd, and all of my Slack buddies. In the words of the *Golden Girls* theme song, thank you for being a friend.

I am grateful for those who made this book a logistical and literal reality, particularly Yolande Sukal. She is a patient, thoughtful, and meticulous graphic designer who has a magical ability to read my mind. The Berklee College of Music provided the time I needed to focus on this book, schools and organizations around the world generously provided financial support, and my newsletter readers continue to give me energy and encouragement to keep going.

To Sam: ><

Credits

Author photos: Michelle Schapiro Photography (Agarwal), Andrew Pannabecker (Blunt), Renata Pedreiro (Ekuni), Vanderbilt University (Fazio), Cheryl Lim (Pan), Paul Brenneman Photography (Sundar), The University of Texas at Austin (Yan), courtesy of the author (Carpenter, Nebel, Rivers, Son)

Figures: Yolande Sukal (Chapters 2, 3, and 8), Veronica Yan (Chapter 4), Kripa Sundar (Chapter 6), Cynthia Nebel (Chapter 7), Roberta Ekuni (Chapter 10)

References

Chapter 1: Retrieval Practice

1. Agarwal, P. K., & Bain, P. B. (2019). *Powerful Teaching: Unleash the Science of Learning.* Jossey-Bass/Wiley.

2. Bates, G., & Shea, J. (2024). Retrieval practice "in the wild": Teachers' reported use of retrieval practice in the classroom. *Mind, Brain, and Education, 18,* 249–257.

3. Pashler, H., Bain, P., Bottge, B., Graesser, A., Koedinger, K., McDaniel, M., and Metcalfe, J. (2007). *Organizing instruction and study to improve student learning.* Institute of Education Sciences, U.S. Department of Education. https://files.eric.ed.gov/fulltext/ED498555.pdf

4. Agarwal, P. K., D'Antonio, L., Roediger, H. L., McDermott, K. B., & McDaniel, M. A. (2014). Classroom-based programs of retrieval practice reduce middle school and high school students' test anxiety. *Journal of Applied Research in Memory and Cognition, 3,* 131–139.

5. Sana, F., Weston, T., & Cepeda, N. J. (2013). Laptop multitasking hinders classroom learning for both users and nearby peers. *Computers & Education, 62,* 24–31.

6. Blake, A. B., Nazarian, M., and Castel, A. D. (2015). The Apple of the mind's eye: Everyday attention, metamemory, and reconstructive memory for the Apple logo. *The Quarterly Journal of Experimental Psychology, 68*(5), 858–865.

7. Roediger, H. L., & Karpicke, J. D. (2006). Test-enhanced learning: Taking memory tests improves long-term retention. *Psychological Science, 17*(3), 249–255.

8. Karpicke, J. D., & Blunt, J. R. (2011). Retrieval practice produces more learning than elaborative studying with concept mapping. *Science, 331*(6018), 772–775.

9. Blunt, J. R., & Karpicke, J. D. (2014). Learning with retrieval-based concept mapping. *Journal of Educational Psychology, 106,* 849–858.

10. Agarwal, P. K., Nunes, L. D., & Blunt, J. R. (2021). Retrieval practice consistently benefits student learning: A systematic review of applied research in schools and classrooms. *Educational Psychology Review, 33,* 1409–1453.

Chapter 2: Early Childhood Education

1. Fazio, L. K. & Marsh, E. J. (2019). Retrieval-based learning in children. *Current Directions in Psychological Science, 28*(2), 111–118.

2. Fritz, C. O., Morris, P. E., Nolan, D., & Singleton, J. (2007). Expanding retrieval practice: An effective aid to preschool children's learning. *Quarterly Journal of Experimental Psychology, 60*(7), 991–1004.

3. Jones, A. C., Wardlow, L., Pan, S. C., Zepeda, C., Heyman, G. D., Dunlosky, J., & Rickard, T. C. (2016). Beyond the rainbow: Retrieval practice leads to better spelling than does rainbow writing. *Educational Psychology Review, 28,* 385–400.

4. Goossens, N. A., Camp, G., Verkoeijen, P. P., Tabbers, H. K., & Zwaan, R. A. (2014). The benefit of retrieval practice over elaborative restudy in primary school vocabulary learning. *Journal of Applied Research in Memory and Cognition, 3*(3), 177–182.

5. Hudson, J. A. (1990). Constructive processing in children's event memory. *Developmental Psychology, 26*(2), 180–187.

6. Memon, A., Wark, L., Bull, R., & Koehnken, G. (1997). Isolating the effects of the cognitive interview techniques. *British Journal of Psychology, 88*(2), 179–197.

7. Adler, S. A., Wilk, A., & Rovee-Collier, C. (2000). Reinstatement versus reactivation effects on active memory in infants. *Journal of Experimental Child Psychology, 75*(2), 93–115.

8. Sheffield, E. G., & Hudson, J. A. (2006). You must remember this: Effects of video and photograph reminders on 18-month-olds' event memory. *Journal of Cognition and Development, 7*(1), 73–93.

9. Hotta, C., Tajika, H., & Neumann, E. (2017). Effects of repeated retrieval on long-term retention in a nonverbal learning task in younger children. *European Journal of Developmental Psychology*, *14*(5), 533–544.

10. Jaeger, A., Eisenkraemer, R. E., & Stein, L. M. (2015). Test-enhanced learning in third-grade children. *Educational Psychology*, *35*(4), 513–521.

11. Lipko-Speed, A., Dunlosky, J., & Rawson, K. A. (2014). Does testing with feedback help grade-school children learn key concepts in science?. *Journal of Applied Research in Memory and Cognition*, *3*(3), 171–176.

12. Karpicke, J. D., Blunt, J. R., Smith, M. A., & Karpicke, S. S. (2014). Retrieval-based learning: The need for guided retrieval in elementary school children. *Journal of Applied Research in Memory and Cognition*, *3*(3), 198–206.

13. Marsh, E. J., Fazio, L. K., & Goswick, A. E. (2012). Memorial consequences of testing school-aged children. *Memory*, *20*(8), 899–906.

14. Carneiro, P., Lapa, A., & Finn, B. (2018). The effect of unsuccessful retrieval on children's subsequent learning. *Journal of Experimental Child Psychology*, *166*, 400–420.

15. Coffman, J. L., Ornstein, P. A., McCall, L. E., & Curran, P. J. (2008). Linking teachers' memory-relevant language and the development of children's memory skills. *Developmental Psychology*, *44*(6), 1640–1654.

16. Grammer, J., Coffman, J. L., & Ornstein, P. (2013). The effect of teachers' memory-relevant language on children's strategy use and knowledge. *Child Development*, *84*(6), 1989–2002.

Chapter 3: Spaced Practice

1. Carpenter, S. K., Pan, S. C., & Butler, A. C. (2022). The science of effective learning with spacing and retrieval practice. *Nature Reviews Psychology*, *1*, 496–511.

2. Carpenter, S. K. (2023). Optimizing learning through retrieval practice and spacing. In R. Tierney, F. Rizvi, & K. Ercikan (Eds.), *International Encyclopedia of Education* (pp. 664–672). Elsevier.

3. Carpenter, S. K., Cepeda, N. J., Rohrer, D., Kang, S. H. K., & Pashler, H. (2012). Using spacing to enhance diverse forms of learning: Review of recent research and implications for instruction. *Educational Psychology Review, 24*, 369–378.

4. McDaniel, M. A., Agarwal, P. K., Huelser, B. J., McDermott, K. B., & Roediger, H. L. III. (2011). Test-enhanced learning in a middle school science classroom: The effects of quiz frequency and placement. *Journal of Educational Psychology, 103*, 399–414.

5. Carpenter, S. K., Pashler, H., & Cepeda, N. J. (2009). Using tests to enhance 8th grade students' retention of U.S. history facts. *Applied Cognitive Psychology, 23*, 760–771.

6. Bloom, K. C., & Shuell, T. J. (1981). Effects of massed and distributed practice on the learning and retention of second-language vocabulary. *The Journal of Educational Research, 74*, 245–248.

7. Kaminske, A. N., Kuepper-Tetzel, C. E., Nebel, C. L., Sumeracki, M. A., & Ryan, S. P. (2020). Transfer: A review for biology and the life sciences. *CBE–Life Sciences Education, 19*(3).

8. Gluckman, M., Vlach, H. A., & Sandhofer, C. M. (2014). Spacing simultaneously promotes multiple forms of learning in children's science curriculum. *Applied Cognitive Psychology, 28*, 266–273.

9. Moulton, C. A. E., Dubrowski, A., MacRae, H., Graham, B., Grober, E., & Reznick, R. (2006). Teaching surgical skills: What kind of practice makes perfect? A randomized, controlled trial. *Annals of Surgery, 244*(3), 400–409.

10. Rohrer, D., Dedrick, R. F., & Agarwal, P. K. (2017). *Interleaved mathematics practice: Giving students a chance to learn what they need to know.* https://www.retrievalpractice.org/library

11. Carpenter, S. K., & Pan, S. C. (2024). Spacing effects in learning and memory. In L. Mickes (Ed.), *Cognitive Psychology of Memory*, Vol. 2 of *Learning and Memory: A Comprehensive Reference*, 3rd edition, J. T. Wixted (Ed.). Oxford Academic Press.

Chapter 4: Interleaving

1. Hall, K. G., Domingues, D. A., & Cavazos, R. (1994). Contextual interference effects with skilled baseball players. *Perceptual and Motor Skills, 78*, 835–841.

2. Sana, F., & Yan, V. X. (2022). Interleaving retrieval practice promotes science learning. *Psychological Science, 33*(5), 782–788.

3. Brunmair, M., & Richter, T. (2019). Similarity matters: A meta-analysis of interleaved learning and its moderators. *Psychological Bulletin, 145*(11), 1029–1052.

4. Yan, V. X., Schuetze, B. A., & Eglington, L. G. (2020). *A review of the interleaving effect: Theories and lessons for future research.* PsyArxiv. https://psyarxiv.com/ur6g7

5. Yan, V. X., Sana, F., & Carvalho, P. F. (2024). No simple solutions to complex problems: Cognitive science principles can guide but not prescribe educational decisions. *Policy Insights from the Behavioral and Brain Sciences, 11*(1), 59–66.

6. Rohrer, D., Dedrick, R. F., & Hartwig, M. K. (2020). The scarcity of interleaved practice in mathematics textbooks. *Educational Psychology Review, 32*(3), 873–883.

7. Yan, V. X., & Schuetze, B. A. (2022). Not just stimuli structure: Sequencing effects in category learning vary by task demands. *Journal of Applied Research in Memory and Cognition, 11*, 218–228.

8. Yan, V. X., Bjork, E. L., & Bjork, R. A. (2016). On the difficulty of mending metacognitive illusions: A priori theories, fluency effects, and misattributions of the interleaving benefit. *Journal of Experimental Psychology: General, 145*(7), 918–933.

Chapter 5: Metacognition

1. Metcalfe, J. (2009). Metacognitive judgments and control of study. *Current Directions in Psychological Science, 18*(3), 159–163.

2. Metcalfe, J., & Finn, B. (2008). Evidence that judgments of learning are causally related to study choice. *Psychonomic Bulletin & Review, 15*(1), 174–179.

3. Kornell, N. (2014). Where is the "meta" in animal metacognition?. *Journal of Comparative Psychology, 128*(2), 143–149.

4. Jirout, J. J., Evans, N. S., & Son, L. K. (2024). Curiosity in children across ages and contexts. *Nature Reviews Psychology, 3*(9), 622–635.

5. Persellin, D. C., & Daniels, M. B. (2023). *A Concise Guide to Teaching with Desirable Difficulties*. Taylor & Francis.

6. Sakulku, J. (2011). The impostor phenomenon. *The Journal of Behavioral Science, 6*(1), 75–97.

7. Son, L. K., & Kornell, N. (2009). Simultaneous decisions at study: Time allocation, ordering, and spacing. *Metacognition and Learning, 4*, 237–248.

8. Ryan, A. M., Pintrich, P. R., & Midgley, C. (2001). Avoiding seeking help in the classroom: Who and why?. *Educational Psychology Review, 13*, 93–114.

9. Zanchetta, M., Junker, S., Wolf, A. M., & Traut-Mattausch, E. (2020). "Overcoming the fear that haunts your success:" The effectiveness of interventions for reducing the impostor phenomenon. *Frontiers in Psychology, 11*, Article 405.

10. Chen, S., & Son, L. K. (2024). High impostors are more hesitant to ask for help. *Behavioral Sciences, 14*(810), 1–17.

Chapter 6: Concept Mapping

1. Ausubel, D. P. (1960). The use of advance organizers in the learning and retention of meaningful verbal material. *Journal of Educational Psychology, 51*(5), 267–272.

2. Adesope, O., Nesbit, J. C., & Sundararajan, N. K. (2021). The mapping principle in multimedia learning. In *The Cambridge Handbook of Multimedia Learning* (pp. 351–359). Cambridge University Press.

3. Nesbit, J. C., & Adesope, O. O. (2006). Learning with concept and knowledge maps: A meta-analysis. *Review of Educational Research, 76*, 413–448.

4. Anastasiou, D., Wirngo, C. N., & Bagos, P. (2024). The effectiveness of concept maps on students' achievement in science: A meta-analysis. *Educational Psychology Review, 36*(2), Article 39.

5. Schroeder, N. L., Nesbit, J. C., Anguiano, C. J., & Adesope, O. O. (2018). Studying and constructing concept maps: A meta-analysis. *Educational Psychology Review, 30*, 431–455.

6. Cañas, A. J., Novak, J. D., & Reiska, P. (2012). Freedom vs. restriction of content and structure during concept mapping: Possibilities and limitations for construction and assessment. *Proceedings of the Fifth International Conference on Concept Mapping, Malta, 2*, 247–257.

7. Hartmeyer, R., Stevenson, M. P., & Bentsen, P. (2018). A systematic review of concept mapping-based formative assessment processes in primary and secondary science education. *Assessment in Education: Principles, Policy & Practice, 25*(6), 598–619.

8. Yue, M., Zhang, M., Zhang, C., & Jin, C. (2017). The effectiveness of concept mapping on development of critical thinking in nursing education: A systematic review and meta-analysis. *Nurse Education Today, 52*, 87–94.

9. Sundararajan, N. K., Adesope, O., & Cavagnetto, A. (2018). The process of collaborative concept mapping in kindergarten and the effect on critical thinking skills. *Journal of STEM Education, 19*(1), 5–13.

10. Wang, Z., Adesope, O., Sundararajan, N. K., & Buckley, P. (2021). Effects of different concept map activities on chemistry learning. *Educational Psychology, 41*(2), 245–260.

11. Sundararajan, N. K. (2022). Concept mapping: A powerful tool for learning. *American Educator, 46*(1), 40–47.

Chapter 7: The Effective Teaching Cycle

1. Sumeracki, M., Nebel, C. L., Kuepper-Tetzel, C., & Kaminske, A. N. (2023). *Ace that test: A student's guide to learning better.* Routledge.

2. Graham, S., & Weiner, B. (1996). Theories and principles of motivation. *Handbook of Educational Psychology.* MacMillan.

3. Willingham, D. T. (2006). How knowledge helps. *American Educator, 30*(1), 30–37.

4. Hopkins, R. F., Lyle, K. B., Hieb, J. L., & Ralston, P. A. (2016). Spaced retrieval practice increases college students' short-and long-term retention of mathematics knowledge. *Educational Psychology Review, 28,* 853–873.

5. Deci, E. L., & Ryan, R. M. (2012). Self-determination theory. *Handbook of Theories of Social Psychology, 1*(20), 416–436.

6. Bandura, A. (1982). Self-efficacy mechanism in human agency. *American Psychologist, 37*(2), 122–147.

7. Van de Pol, J., Volman, M., & Beishuizen, J. (2010). Scaffolding in teacher–student interaction: A decade of research. *Educational Psychology Review, 22,* 271–296.

8. Kalyuga, S. (2007). Expertise reversal effect and its implications for learner-tailored instruction. *Educational Psychology Review, 19,* 509–539.

9. Carpenter, S. K., Cepeda, N. J., Rohrer, D., Kang, S. H., & Pashler, H. (2012). Using spacing to enhance diverse forms of learning: Review of recent research and implications for instruction. *Educational Psychology Review, 24,* 369–378.

10. Abel, M., & Bäuml, K. H. T. (2020). Would you like to learn more? Retrieval practice plus feedback can increase motivation to keep on studying. *Cognition, 201,* 104316.

Chapter 8: Transfer of Learning

1. Barnett, S. M., & Ceci, S. J. (2002). When and where do we apply what we learn?: A taxonomy for far transfer. *Psychological Bulletin, 128*(4), 612–637.

2. Pan, S. C., & Rickard, T. C. (2018). Transfer of test-enhanced learning: Meta-analytic review and synthesis. *Psychological Bulletin, 144*(7), 710–756.

3. Hinze, S. R., Wiley, J., & Pellegrino, J. W. (2013). The importance of constructive comprehension processes in learning from tests. *Journal of Memory and Language, 69*(2), 151–164.

4. Agarwal, P. K. (2019). Retrieval practice and Bloom's taxonomy: Do students need fact knowledge before higher order learning? *Journal of Educational Psychology, 111*, 189–209.

5. McDaniel, M. A., Thomas, R. C., Agarwal, P. K., McDermott, K. B., & Roediger, H. L. (2013). Quizzing in middle-school science: Successful transfer performance on classroom exams. *Applied Cognitive Psychology, 27*, 360–372.

6. Butler, A. C., Godbole, N., & Marsh, E. J. (2013). Explanation feedback is better than correct answer feedback for promoting transfer of learning. *Journal of Educational Psychology, 105*, 290–298.

7. Gick, M. L., & Holyoak, K. J. (1980). Analogical problem solving. *Cognitive Psychology, 12*(3), 306–355.

8. Corral, D., Carpenter, S. K., & St. Hilaire, K. J. (2023). The effects of retrieval versus study on analogical problem solving. *Psychonomic Bulletin & Review, 30*(5), 1954–1965.

Chapter 9: Bringing It Together

1. Blake, A. B., Nazarian, M., and Castel, A. D. (2015). The Apple of the mind's eye: Everyday attention, metamemory, and reconstructive memory for the Apple logo. *The Quarterly Journal of Experimental Psychology, 68*(5), 858–865.

2. Finn, B., & Tauber, S. K. (2015). When confidence is not a signal of knowing: How students' experiences and beliefs about processing fluency can lead to miscalibrated confidence. *Educational Psychology Review, 27*, 567–586.

3. Sana, F., Forrin, N. D., Sharma, M., Dubljevic, T., Ho, P., Jalil, E., & Kim, J. A. (2020). Optimizing the efficacy of learning objectives through pretests. *CBE—Life Sciences Education, 19*(3), 1–10.

4. Tullis, J. G., & Goldstone, R. L. (2020). Why does peer instruction benefit student learning?. *Cognitive Research: Principles and Implications, 5*(15), 1–12.

5. Overono, A. L. (in press). Exploring the impact of required justifications in multiple-choice elaboration questions on student experiences and performance. *Journal of the Scholarship of Teaching and Learning*.

6. Hartwig, M. K., & Dunlosky, J. (2012). Study strategies of college students: Are self-testing and scheduling related to achievement?. *Psychonomic Bulletin & Review, 19*, 126–134.

7. Rivers, M. L. (2021). Metacognition about practice testing: A review of learners' beliefs, monitoring, and control of test-enhanced learning. *Educational Psychology Review, 33*, 823–862.

8. McDaniel, M. A., & Einstein, G. O. (2023). How to teach powerful strategies so that students self-regulate their use: The KBCP framework. In *In their own words: What scholars and teachers want you to know about why and how to apply the science of learning in your academic setting* (pp. 365–377). Society for the Teaching of Psychology.

9. Rivers, M. L. (2023). Test experience, direct instruction, and their combination promote accurate beliefs about the testing effect. *Journal of Intelligence, 11*(7), 147.

Chapter 10: Neuromyths Debunked

1. Sazaka, L. S. R., Hermida, M. J., & Ekuni, R. (2024). Where did preservice teachers, teachers, and the general public learn neuromyths?

Insights to support teacher training. *Trends in Neuroscience and Education, 36*, Article 100235.

2. Macdonald, K., Germine, L., Anderson, A., Christodoulou, J., & McGrath, L. M. (2017). Dispelling the myth: Training in education or neuroscience decreases but does not eliminate beliefs in neuromyths. *Frontiers in Psychology, 8*, Article 1314.

3. van Dijk, W., & Lane, H. B. (2018). The brain and the U.S. education system: Perpetuation of neuromyths. *Exceptionality, 28*(1), 16–29.

4. Ekuni, R., & Pompéia, S. (2016). The impact of scientific dissemination in the perpetuation of neuromyths in education. *Revista da Biologia, 15*(1), 21–28.

5. Sazaka, L. S. R., Hermida, M. J., & Ekuni, R. (2024). Where did pre-service teachers, teachers, and the general public learn neuromyths? Insights to support teacher training. *Trends in Neuroscience and Education*, Article 100235.

6. Torrijos-Muelas, M., González-Víllora, S., & Bodoque-Osma, A. R. (2021). The persistence of neuromyths in the educational settings: A systematic review. *Frontiers in Psychology, 11*, Article 591923.

7. Pomerance, L., Greenberg, J., & Walsh, K. (2016). *Learning about learning: What every new teacher needs to know*. National Council on Teacher Quality. https://files.eric.ed.gov/fulltext/ED570861.pdf

8. Luiz, I., Lindell, A. K., & Ekuni, R. (2020). Neurophilia is stronger for educators than students in Brazil. *Trends in Neuroscience and Education, 20*, Article 100136.

9. De Bruyckere, P., Kirschner, P. A., & Hulshof, C. D. (2015). *Urban Myths About Learning and Education*. Academic Press.

10. Agarwal, P. K., & Bain, P. B. (2019). *Powerful Teaching: Unleash the Science of Learning*. Jossey-Bass/Wiley.

11. Rousseau, L. (2021). Interventions to dispel neuromyths in educational settings—A review. *Frontiers in Psychology, 12*, 719692.

www.ingramcontent.com/pod-product-compliance
Lightning Source LLC
Chambersburg PA
CBHW020505030426
42337CB00011B/240